Radical Criminology

issue three ★ winter 2014

ISSN: 1929-7904
ISBN: 978-0615965796

a publication of the
Critical Criminology Working Group
at Kwantlen Polytechnic University
(12666 72 Avenue, Surrey, BC V3W 2M8)
www.radicalcriminology.org

punctum books ✶ brooklyn, ny
www.punctumbooks.com

★ Radical Criminology ★ Issue 3 ★ January 2014 ★ ISSN 1929-7904

General Editor: Jeff Shantz

Production Editor: PJ Lilley

Advisory Board: Olga Aksyutina, Institute for African Studies of Russian Academy of Sciences, Moscow; **Davina Bhandar** (Trent U.); **Jeff Ferrell** (Texas Christian U.); **Hollis Johnson** (Kwantlen Polytechnic U.); **Michael J. Lynch** (U. of South Florida); **Mike CK Ma** (Kwantlen Polytechnic U.); **Lisa Monchalin** (Kwantlen Polytechnic U.); **Heidi Rimke** (U.Winnipeg); **Jeffrey Ian Ross** (U.Baltimore); **Herman Schwendinger,** independent scholar

cover art: Fanny Aishaa

layout & design: PJ Lilley

Unless otherwise stated, contributions express the opinions of their writers and are not (necessarily) those of the Editors or Advisory Board. Please visit our website for more information.

★ Contact Us ★

email: editors@radicalcriminology.org

website: http://journal.radicalcriminology.org

Mailing address: Kwantlen Polytechnic University, ATTN: Jeff Shantz, Dept. of Criminology 12666 72 Avenue I Surrey, BC, Canada V3W 2M8

★

In this period of state-sponsored austerity and suppression of resistance there is a great need for criminologists to speak out and act against state violence, state-corporate crime, and the growth of surveillance regimes and the prison-industrial complex. Criminologists also have a role to play in advancing alternatives to current regimes of regulation and punishment. In light of current social struggles against neoliberal capitalism, and as an effort to contribute positively to those struggles, the Critical Criminology Working Group at Kwantlen Polytechnic University in Vancouver has initiated this open access journal, *Radical Criminology*. We now welcome contributions. (See back page or our website for more details.)

Future issues might include:
Prison Abolition • Anti-colonialism • Resistance to Borders & Securitization • Surveillance and the Digital Panopticon • Anti-capitalism & Corporate Crime • the Military-Industrial Complex

This is not simply a project of critique, but is geared toward a praxis of struggle, insurgence and practical resistance.

★

Readers are welcome, and contributors are requested to keep in touch by signing up at
http://journal.radicalcriminology.org

Our website uses the Open Journal System,
developed by the Public Knowledge Project at Simon
Fraser University:

journal.radicalcriminology.org

✳

Inside

insurgencies /

book reviews /

Editorial:
Neither Justice nor Crime
(We are all Criminals Now)

We have entered a period in which it must finally be recognized and admitted that criminal justice systems in Western liberal democracies are neither, in any real or meaningful way, about justice nor, even, about crime.

While it has perhaps long been recognized, at least by those subjected to its numerous inequities and biases and excesses (among critical theorists and certainly among the oppressed) that criminal justice is not about justice (this awareness represented in oppositional voices, particularly by poor and racialized communities that speak of "injustice system" or notions of "just us"), it is a more recently glimpsed (perhaps only partly) reality that criminal justice systems are not now (if ever) directed at addressing (in some vague way, never mind *stopping*) crime. They do not even live up to that minimal claim to legitimation.

This emerging awareness is based in the recognition that most criminal justice system activity is not even taken up with dealing with actual crimes (let alone social harms), except in the minimal degree necessary to maintain some legitimizing capacities. Rather, most criminal justice system activity is involved in two areas: first, in dealing with administration and administrative breaches; and second, in surveillance and punishment of people not engaged in criminal activity.

As Aiyanas Ormond, in this issue, points out, approximately 21 percent of criminal justice system activity is directed toward administrative offenses in the Canadian context. These include failures to appear, missed meetings, unpaid fines, etc. rather than actual "crimes" (associated with any social harms). Ormond suggests that the system is driven by a class-based

7

process of "crime mining" in which low level, or entirely harmless occurrences, typically survival strategies of the poor, are increasingly criminalized or illegalized, brought within the system for processing as a means for keeping public funds circulating into the system agencies and institutions at a time when actual crime rates are dropping.

Even more dramatically, and perhaps foreboding (and more disturbing for the middle strata and more comfortable) is the fact that much of the system's resources are directed at the surveillance, criminalization and punishment of people *who have committed no crime*. This includes the broad range of criminalizing practices deployed against protesters and others caught up on the streets during protest events—people who are arrested and detained simply because they are present in areas (where they might live or have jobs) that the state is securing for global economic and political elites (as at meetings of the G8 and G20 or World Trade Organization, etc.).

In Toronto during the G20 meetings of 2010, for example, around 1300 people were arrested, the largest mass arrest in Canadian history, and detained throughout the G20 meeting period—despite having done nothing wrong (reflected in the fact that almost all were released without charge after the meetings concluded). Many were not even protesters—quite a few were workers simply heading to or from their jobs. A large proportion of detainees were arrested through so-called kettling practices in which police trap crowds in alleyways or side streets (regardless of what individuals in the crowd were doing beforehand) and refuse to let them leave. In these cases everyone on a street is viewed as, treated, as, rendered, a criminal. They are all made illegal. Even where they have done *nothing* to cause concern or harm.

Beyond this are the variety of associational laws generated over the last two decades that criminalize people, again not for any actions they have engaged in, simply for having some sort of, often tenuous, vague, or meaningless "connection" or "association" with a group or collective that the state dislikes. In Canada, well before the 9/11 attacks provided the statist justification for all manner of egregious laws, the government of the day passed anti-gang legislation that allowed the state to arrest, detain, and charge people, as well as seizing their assets, if they had some gang association. Typically the law served only to target rather low level participants. It was not long before the Chief of Police in Toronto (now a federal government minister) attempted to have an anti-poverty group known for direct action politics, the Ontario Coalition Against Poverty, declared a gang, members arrested, office resources seized. While the Chief was thwarted in that effort, after 9/11 the anti-terror laws passed almost immediately afterward extended the associational legislation for use against people having, again vague, association with supposed terrorist groups. Incredibly, evidence of association in these cases can consist of a little as wearing a patch with a terror group symbol on your clothing or selling a newspaper from a labeled group.

These associational policies represent a significant dismantling of central aspects of liberal democratic legal systems. They do away with foundations of due process: disclosure of evidence, assumptions of innocence. In cases like security certificates, legal instruments in Canada that allow the state to arrest and detain people without cause, for unlimited periods, without evidence, and without public hearings, even *habeas corpus* is jeopardized. Such legislation renders criminological staples of *actus rea* and *mens rea* entirely meaningless.

While the state focus on activists—organizers, protesters, and any oppositional forces—is not new (and forms a large part of the basis for state formation in capitalist liberal democracies), what is a significant recent development is that state control practices, as in NSA spying or surveillance activities for example, are now directed at regular folks—at everyone, even the citizens who most accept state claims to criminal justice legitimacy.

Criminologists, rather than posing as mere analysts of criminal justice systems who, even as critics, accept that, even if they cannot dispense justice, they at least deal with crime, (while perhaps offering suggestions for improvement or questioning the relationship to justice along the way), must take up the new pressing task of shifting the focus and foundation of the discipline.

We must stop pursuing the study of a chimera—of something that does not exist (or else move our discipline to the realm of mythic studies or fantasy). We certainly must toss aside our taken-for-granted assumptions about the discipline's central organizational object of study. If the criminal justice system is involved neither in addressing crime nor in securing justice, what then is its current character and foundation? In the current period, the so-called criminal justice system is largely about the circulation of social wealth in a manner that deprives the poor and enriches those with greater economic privilege. Indeed, as criminologists we might well shift to organizational analysis of self-perpetuating bureaucracies or profit-making tendencies to accumulation within bureaucracies.

Criminal justice systems as sprawling bureaucracies are directed, as all bureaucracies are, at self preservation and managed growth. They tend to expand (in size and in reach). They are redistributors of wealth upwards. They take resources from the working classes and deploy it upwards toward the more privileged (lawyers, judges, politicians, private capital).

But the criminal justice system serves another important function. And that is to render any and all who might challenge its position and privilege (and the position of the status quo it upholds and profits from) as against the law, as illegal. Even more, though, in the current period the system serves to make suspect, to survey, to track and contain, to criminalize, and to warn even those who do not oppose. These become the common characteristics of everyday life within liberal democracies (which are rendered perhaps post-liberal non-democracies).

Critical theorists such as Jeff Reiman have incisively shown that criminal justice systems in capitalist liberal democracies are not designed to deliver justice. Reiman has shown instead that the system works rather to shift attention away from the social harms of elites and to focus on the crimes of the working classes. This reinforces a narrative that describes social harm as coming from non-elites—the so-called dangerous classes to be feared and regulated.

Yet this approach is incomplete and does not go far enough. The issue today that criminology must contend with is that the criminal justice system is not maintained by a focus on actual crime (whether working class or not). And the system, in its surveillance functions especially, is directed at a generalized *non-criminality*. This is a key transformation.

We are all illegal now. We are all criminals, resources to be mined and manipulated to fulfill the self-perpetuating drives of accumulating systems. And, what is really in play, we are all potential media of exchange for systems designed fundamentally to accumulate capital and redistribute resources (from bottom to top) in a self-aggrandizing fashion. But we must be converted to the proper currency and the new criminalizing practices achieve this.

In this context we must give up all claims to be objective, neutral analysts (while blithely deluding ourselves that what we study, as a criminal justice system, actually exists). If those threatened with or subjected to repression, surveillance, criminalization, and/or state violence are portrayed as—and treated as—insurgents (as threats to the systemic status quo) then criminologists, as those who are supposed to understand the workings of these systems, have a responsibility to stand with the insurgents against the forces of criminalization. We must be insurgents ourselves. Criminology must, in recognizing and honestly naming, systems of repression must also be an insurgent practice.

Our criminology must be an insurgent criminology. That is, it must be a criminology in and of active struggles, active revolt, against states, and capital, and their criminal justice systems; a criminology that rises against, that seeks to abolish instituted authorities.

Jeff Shantz, December 2013, Surrey (Newton), B.C.
(unceded coast salish territories)

[features]

Heinous Crime or Acceptable Violence? The Disparate Framing of Femicides in Hawai'i

NICOLAS CHAGNON

ABSTRACT

Violence against women is a pervasive social problem, yet it is under-reported in the press. Scholars have long critiqued media for flawed coverage of this crime. Yet, few studies have specifically examined femicides using an intersectional framework. This study does that, examining femicide coverage in Hawaii's two major dailies—*The Honolulu Advertiser* and *Star-Bulletin* —between 2000 and 2008. Findings indicate that Hawaii's newspapers frame femicides disparately—as an unacceptable social problem, or as routine, acceptable violence. This disparate framing is accomplished through the clustering of patriarchal, racialized, and class-based discourses. Considering Hawaii's distinct racial/ethnic diversity, racialized discourses in this sample were particularly thought provoking, employing insidious and nuanced racialized markers to 'other' various groups. Findings regarding these racialized discourses may be generalizable to analyses of 'post-racial' discourse on an increasingly diverse mainland.

INTRODUCTION

Femicides are one of the most troubling, and common, forms of homicide in Hawaii. Yet, Hawaii's press largely fails to communicate this significance. They sometimes cover femicides defensibly, problematizing this crime and humanizing victims. Unfortunately, such coverage is exceptional. In this article, I discuss how coverage tends to employ two disparate frames for femicides—one, the 'social problem' frame, cultivates sympathy for the victim, gives some context, and problematizes domestic violence. The other (and more common), the 'acceptable violence' frame, does the near opposite, reporting in a routinized, simplistic manner. These frames are built upon clustered and intersecting patriarchal, racialized, and class-based discourses. Thus, they provide the illusion of problematizing domestic violence but actually work to perpetuate existing hierarchies built upon class, race, and gender divisions.

For decades, scholars have pointed out that media representations of crime exaggerate crimes committed by the poor and marginalized, and often minimalize the crimes of the wealthy and white (Chiricos and Eschholz 2002; Gilliam and Iyengar 2000; Grover and Soothill 1996; Hall et al. 1978; Herman and Chomsky 2002; Mason 2006; McMullan 2006). Feminist scholars have added to this discussion, pointing out that news on violence against women (VAW) is particularly troubling because it conceals the pervasiveness and patriarchal roots of this violence (Benedict 1993; Dragiewicz 2011; Meyers 1994; Richards, Gillespie, and Smith 2011). Furthermore, some scholars point out that crime news functions as hegemonic ideology, which not only obscures the character of crime, but also reinforces existing power structures and fundamental inequalities (Hall et al. 1978; Herman and Chomsky 2002; Jewkes 2010; Meyers 1994).

Feminist scholars have produced copious research on VAW in the media. However, there is less research which specifically focuses on femicides; enlists both qualitative and quantitative analyses; and examines intersectional discourses (Richards, Gillespie, and Smith 2011). In this article I discuss findings from a mixed qualitative and quantitative analysis of femicide articles in Hawaii's two major dailies—the *Honolulu Advertis-*

er and *Star-Bulletin,* between 2000-2008. In the following sections I review the existing literature on crime and VAW in the media, discuss Hawaii as a distinct context for such a study (especially in regards to race), provide a methodological overview, outline key story components, discuss how these themes cluster to form the social problem and acceptable violence frames, and conclude by briefly summarizing my argument and discussing its theoretical relevance.

LITERATURE REVIEW

PATRIARCHAL MEDIA

Critics have long pointed out that media representations of crime are unrealistic, giving the public a distorted impression of crime in Western society (Best 1990; Hall et al. 1978; Mason 2006; Sacco 1995; Surette 2007). Feminist scholars have echoed such concerns, pointing out flaws in press coverage of VAW in particular (Benedict 1993, 1993; Bullock and Cubert 2002; Dragiewicz 2011; Kozol 1995; Meyers 1994; Schwartz and DeKeseredy 1993; Stanko 2000; Taylor 2009; Websdale and Alvarez 1998). Such flawed coverage hides the pervasiveness and patterns of VAW, under-problematizing it. Thus, since VAW is a pillar of patriarchy, whether intentionally or not, media support and reproduce patriarchal arrangements (Dragiewicz 2011; Meyers 1994; Ogle and Batton 2009; Walby 1989; Websdale and Alvarez 1998).

Prior to the 1970s, media ignored domestic violence, treating it as a private matter (Kozol 1995). Today, they have moved beyond such ignorance, reporting on it. However, news reports continue to cover VAW in a partial and decontextualized manner. Howe (1997) contends the media repeatedly 're-discover' VAW, treating is as a novel, rather than a historically persistent, phenomenon. Press reports often ignore the prevalence of rape and domestic violence, failing to contextualize these acts as a serious social problem (Benedict 1993; Meyers 1994; Richards, Gillespie, and Smith 2011). This is manifest in at least two clear patterns. First, the occurrence of this violence throughout various strata of society is rarely acknowledged; instead press reports present VAW as if it is located largely in a marginalized underclass (Grover and Soothill 1996; Websdale and Alvarez 1998). Second, the press often ignores patterns of escalation in wife and partner abuse (Bullock and Cubert 2002; Websdale and Alvarez 1998). Such abuse is generally covered only when it is fatal (or nearly so); such fatalities are presented as stand-alone incidents, rather than the crescendo of escalating violence.

Media coverage often blames raped and battered women for their own victimhood, while excusing some men for their crimes (Benedict 1993; Bullock and Cubert 2002; Meyers 1994; Taylor 2009; Websdale and Alvarez 1998). Victim-blaming themes include questioning the victim's choice of clothing; supposedly flirtatious behavior and/or sexual history; or emphasizing a victim's reluctance to leave an abuser, among other themes (Benedict 1993; Taylor 2009). As Benedict (1993) points out, one might say the media construct a dichotomy among sex victims, between virgins and vamps—chaste, innocent victims who accord with hegemonic assumptions about female behavior and identity; and lascivious and/or rebellious women who deserve what they get. More generally, some scholars have pointed out that media representations construct worthy and unworthy female victims (Chancer 1994; Meyers 1994; Schwartz and DeKeseredy 1993). This worthiness is both determined by the victim's identity and behavior and that of her attacker. Powerful and privileged men's status generally mitigates their culpability in media coverage (Benedict 1993; Meyers 1994). News often frames VAW committed by powerful men as the result of factors beyond offenders' control, such as mental illness or substance abuse (Richards, Gillespie, and Smith 2011; Taylor 2009; Websdale and Alvarez 1998). Postmurder suicides (or attempts) by offenders also often lead to offender-sympathetic coverage. These murder-suicides are often framed by reports as mutual tragedies, rather than acts of domestic violence (Websdale and Alvarez 1998). Taylor (2009) conceptualizes victim maligning and sympathy for offenders as direct and indirect blaming, respectively. Direct blaming impugns the victim. Indirect blaming essentially sympathizes with the offender, deflecting attention from the victim's suffering.

Even the press' reporting techniques limit recognition and understanding of VAW. For example, terms like 'domestic violence' or 'partner violence' conceal the fact that this is over-whelmingly abuse of women by men (Dragiewicz 2011; Mey-ers 1994; Websdale and Alvarez 1998). Furthermore, the com-mon use of passive voice can limit press construction of vio-lence. For example, Henley, Miller, and Beazley (1995) found that media reports of VAW often use passive voice, which causes readers to ascribe less harm to these crimes. Additional-ly, reporters often focus on minute details of cases, such as gun calibres or wound descriptions, which tell the reader very little about VAW as a social problem (Bullock and Cubert 2002; Websdale and Alvarez 1998). Websdale and Alvarez (1998) call this 'forensic reporting,' while Bullock and Cubert (2002) call it the 'police frame.' Ultimately, this mode of reporting fo-cuses readers' attention on the details of specific cases, while obscuring thematic patterns of VAW.

In sum, many scholars argue, the above-mentioned patterns of coverage amount to support for and reproduction of patri-archy on the part of media (Dragiewicz 2011; Meyers 1994; Websdale and Alvarez 1998). By ignoring and/or limiting pub-lic understanding of a pillar of patriarchy (VAW), the media ensure that this social problem will be under-addressed and pa-triarchal conditions will persist (Walby 1989).

INTERSECTIONAL ANALYSES

Feminist analyses of VAW often use an intersectional analytic perspective, which looks at systems of race, class, and gender simultaneously (Benedict 1993; Chancer 1994; Meyers 1994). Such an analysis allows for a better understanding of the inter-relations among multiple stratifying social systems (Burgess-Proctor 2006). For example, Meyers' (1994) case study of one murder-suicide shows how coverage used the race and class of both the victim and killer, in concert with victim blaming, to minimalize the offender's culpability and imply victim culpa-bility. In a similar study, analyzing two infamous cases—the Central Park jogger and New Bedford bar gang rapes—Chancer (1994) documents the disparate coverage granted to an upper-class white and a lower-class Portuguese victim. The former was celebrated as a martyr, while the latter was demonized as a seductress. Furthermore, coverage villified the attackers of the white victim, while excusing those of the other.

An intersectional perspective shows that media reports not only treat victims differentially, but also the men who attack them. Specifically, some scholars have pointed out that news reports frame non-white and/or lower class men's violent acts against women in a manner holding them more accountable, than white, rich men (Grover and Soothill 1996; Kozol 1995; McDonald 1999). In fact, Grover and Soothill (1996) claim that media representations frame sex crimes as largely perpetrated by a 'murderous underclass' of marginalized men.

Essentially, these scholars have shown that media coverage of VAW is not monolithically encoded with patriarchal messages. Instead, multifarious discourses, contingent upon racialized and class-based themes, produce textured frames of VAW. This coverage is basically more sympathetic to white/and or economically privileged victims and offenders, while portraying non-whites and/or the lower class in a stigmatizing manner.

INTERSECTIONAL HEGEMONY

This intersectional perspective, Meyers (1994) argues, can be used to refine hegemony theories. Classical studies in hegemony are founded on class-based analysis (see Hall et al. 1978). As originally articulated by Gramsci (1971), cultural hegemony is the process by which the capitalist class secures the voluntary consent of other classes, by constructing, and imposing upon the people, a cultural ideology that naturalizes the capitalist class structure and economic modality. However, ideologies which work to reproduce existing structures do not only apply to class (Meyers 1994). Patriarchy and racial stratification are also built and maintained through the help of supporting ideologies (Ogle and Batton 2009).

Furthermore, hegemonic ideology (like hegemonic structure) is flexible, capable of absorbing and/or coopting challenging discourses (Gitlin 2003; Hall et al. 1978). Hegemonic ideologies are not static, yet evolve to give the impression of a progressive, egalitarian society. Beyond this, while hegemony may be global, it also has localized iterations (Connell and Messerschmidt 2005). Thus, a theory of hegemony, which accounts for multiple systems of oppression, historical changes to the hegemonic order, and localized varieties, is likely a clearer lens for making sense of reality. One might call such a theory 'intersectional hegemony.' This paper operates from the assumption that femicide coverage in Hawaii constitutes localized, intersectional hegemonic ideology, the implications of which will be discussed in the conclusion.

THE PRESENT STUDY

CONTEXT

Femicides are particularly problematic in Hawaii. Though, Hawaii has a relatively low violent crime rate,[1] a large proportion of this crime occurs within intimate partnerships (Silent Witness 2006). Hawaii crime statistics demonstrate this significance. There were 268 homicides in the state during the sampling time frame (2000-2008), with 81 female homicide victims and 88 homicides in which victims and offenders were intimate partners or nuclear family members (U.S. Department of Justice 2010). Forty-eight of these were femicides, making up about 59% of female homicides, and nearly 18% of total homicides in the state (Kline 2010).

Perhaps more important (at least theoretically) than its crime patterns, is Hawaii's diversity. The state's racial and ethnic makeup is far different from most mainland locations (Okamura 2008; Rohrer 2008; Sorensen, Wood, and Prince 2003). Whites are not the racial majority. In fact, Asians comprise the largest racial group in Hawaii, making up 38.8 % of the population. Whites make up 30.2 % of the population; Hawaiian and Pacific Islanders make up 9.2 %; Hispanic and Latinos 9.0 %; and blacks, 3.2 % (U.S. Census Bureau 2010). A significant portion (18.0 %) of the population identifies as multi-racial. Furthermore, significant portions of the state's population identify with dozens of different ethnicities or nationalities (Sorenson, Wood & Prince 2003).

This distinct diversity is theoretically useful for understanding the fluidity of racial construction. Racial and ethnic distinc-

---

[1] Hawaii ranked 36th in the nation in 2006, with a violent crime rate of 281 per 100,000 persons (U.S. Census Bureau 2006) and the 2009 murder rate was 1.7 per 100,000, about a third of the national average of 5.0 per 100,000 (U.S. Department of Justice 2010).

tions in Hawaii are not necessarily made through a white/non-white binary (Okamura 2008). Furthermore, at least partially because Hawaii is comprised of significant proportions of various Asian groups (e.g. Chinese, Japanese, Filipino, Korean, etc.), markers such as nationality, immigration status, and immigration cohort play more integral roles in the construction of racial and ethnic hierarchies than they might on the mainland. For example, many residents employ a pan-ethnic identity, the 'local' identity, in a manner that overshadows their racial/ethnic heritage (Okamura 1992). While this identity is not an ethnicity per se, it entails some of the markers of ethnicity (e.g. common rituals, foods, etc.), adding complexity to the construction of ethnic hierarchies in Hawaii.

Popular discourses often characterize Hawaii as a racial utopia (Rohrer 2008). However, these discourses mask insidious, yet powerful tensions between whites and non-whites. For example, demographic statistics elide the fact that though they are not a numeric majority, whites still hold most of the political and economic capital in Hawaii. More generally, the ubiquity of racial-utopia discourses creates a social atmosphere in which many residents (and journalists) downplay actual racial/ethnic inequality, while emphasizing a (at least somewhat) fictitious harmony (Okamura 2008; Rohrer 2008). Hawaii's diversity and the discourses regarding it make the state a ripe case for illuminating alternate constructions of racial/ethnic hierarchies.

DATA

The data for this study come from newspaper articles published in Hawaii's two major dailies, *The Honolulu Advertiser* and *The Star-Bulletin.* Before the papers merged in 2010, the *Advertiser's* circulation was approximately 209,000 and the *Star-Bulletin's* was approximately 64,000. I specifically chose to use local, rather than national media, because national media tend to only report on the most uncommon and/or gruesome femicides (Ryan, Anastario, and DaCunha 2006).

Specifically, I examined stories on cases occurring from 2000-2008[2], which were published during that period. This time period is slightly longer than the period examined by previous femicide studies (Bullock and Cubert 2002; Richards, Gillespie, and Smith 2011; Taylor 2009; Websdale and Alvarez 1998). To find articles, I used an approach similar to that of Richards, Gillespie, and Smith (2011), searching the Hawaii Newspaper Indexes database for the names of each victim and offender involved in the 48 femicides during the sampling timeframe (Kline 2010). This search yielded a list of 650 potentially appropriate articles, which, because of limitations with the newspaper index, is likely as close as possible to what Lundman (2003) calls the 'universe of coverage.' This list is several times larger than the samples of many earlier studies (Bullock and Cubert 2002; Richards, Gillespie, and Smith 2011; Taylor 2009; Websdale and Alvarez 1998). To make the sample more manageable I used a random number generator to select 150 articles from the 650-item sampling frame. Twenty-eight articles were ultimately deemed inappropriate. Most of these articles were written too early in the investigation of the crime for the reporter to identify the identity of the offender, or the victim-offender relationship. Thus, I analyzed a total of 122 articles, averaging 391.9 words. Because, there were more articles in the sample than there were femicides occurring during the sampling time frame, some, but not all, cases are featured in more than one article in the sample.

ANALYSIS

Using the Microsoft Access 2007 database software, I performed all analysis myself, with each article serving as the unit of analysis. To do this, I used a 58-item content analysis scheme that included both quantitative and qualitative measures. This coding scheme was initially derived from key themes from previous research. For example, Taylor's (2009) study informed my measures of victim blaming and Websdale and Alvarez' (1998) study informed my investigation of foren-

---

[2] I selected this period to provide contemporary data. However, I cut off data before their merger, because my wider analysis involved comparing the two outlets. Including data after the merger would have confounded such an analysis.

sic reporting. A sample coding scheme, including the variables specifically related to the research discussed here, is provided in Appendix 1.

I analyzed these data using an iterative procedure akin to a constant comparative method (Charmaz 2006; Glaser and Strauss 1967). I performed several waves of coding on each article, refining codes and recoding for emergent themes. Several key variables emerged, expanding the scheme from 47 items initially, to 58. For example, the role of temporary restraining orders (TROs) was emphasized in many articles. I had not anticipated this being a salient theme at the outset, but added a variable to cover this, and recoded dozens of articles.

I also used some basic quantitative measures to analyze my data. Instead of inferential statistics, I used frequencies and percentages to confirm my conclusions arising from qualitative analyses. In the following sections of this paper I use these numbers to illustrate the quantitative substance of my qualitative findings.

Findings

Simplifying and Decontextualizing Story Components

I this section, I will first discuss key story components, the presence or absence of which works to problematize femicides or obfuscate them. Following previous research, I argue these components simplify and decontextualize femicides, masking their status as patriarchal products (Meyers 1994; Websdale and Alvarez 1998). Because of this, coverage provides support for, rather than a challenge to, the patriarchal status quo. Thus, they constitute patriarchal discourse. After discussing story components as patriarchal discourse, I will discuss how these components coincide with representations of class and racializing discourses constructing disparate femicides frames—the social problem and acceptable violence frames—which work to not only support patriarchy, but also simultaneously perpetuate hierarchies based on class and race.

As other researchers have argued, the first step in meaningful femicide coverage is identifying the crime as domestic violence (Gillespie et al. 2013). In this sample, less than a third of articles (30.3%) characterize femicides as domestic violence. Many articles merely alluded to this, referring euphemistically to 'marital troubles' or 'domestic disputes,' sometimes implying mutual combat. Furthermore, very few tied specific acts of domestic violence to other similar acts. Only about 10% of articles made any linkages between multiple incidents. Additionally, echoing results from previous studies, official sources were overwhelmingly favored over others in this sample (Bullock and Cubert 2002; Richards, Gillespie, and Smith 2011; Websdale and Alvarez 1998). Nearly all articles (97.5%) cited official sources (police or prosecutors). Previous studies have argued that stories citing officials often fail to characterize an incident as domestic violence because police are sometimes unaware of previous abuse and/or focus on the details of cases rather than the broader context (Gillespie et al. 2013; Taylor 2009). On the other hand, family members and domestic violence experts are better equipped than officials to identify femicides as domestic violence because of, respectively, their familiarity with the victim's relationship with the offender or this genre of crime. A minority of articles employed these sources —36.9 % of stories used family members or friends while advocates or experts were cited in only 7.3 % of articles.

Instead of identifying the crimes as domestic violence, articles often engaged in forensic reporting (Websdale and Alvarez 1998). About half of the sample (47.5%) featured forensic reporting. These stories focused on the minutiae of incidents, such as makes of vehicles, exact timelines, body positions, weapon descriptions, etc. For example, one report read, "[the victim] was stabbed 16 times in the bedroom of a house the couple shared on Kahaha Street in Kalihi. She was stabbed in the heart and lungs, the thighs and on her face and arms, and had defensive wounds on her hands." Forensic details often made up the totality of articles. Such stories largely mystified, rather than problematized, femicides.

Forensic reporting often accompanied the use of ambiguous headlines that concealed the nature of the crime (Henley, Miller, & Beazley 1995). For example, one article, documenting a murder-suicide read, "Dead couple identified." This title obscures the fact that a man killed his wife; one might believe this was an accident from the title. Another headline read, "Suspect arrested in stabbing death of South Kona woman." This headline acknowledges the murder, but not the victim-offender relationship. Clearly, headlines are not the totality of content, but they set the tone for the article. Beyond this, they suggest reporters are reluctant to emphasize domestic violence. Use of these misleading headlines was pervasive, occurring in 71.3% of the articles.

The above-mentioned themes obscure femicides-as-domestic violence through omission of contextualizing material. Media coverage may also obscure these crimes by shifting blame from offender to victim (Taylor 2009). Victim blaming was not as common as the preceding themes, but was present. Like previous studies, my analysis revealed significant victim-blaming, both direct and indirect, occurring in 18.8% of articles (Benedict 1993; Bullock and Cubert 2002; Meyers 1994; Richards, Gillespie, and Smith 2011; Taylor 2009). Various victim-blaming discourses were present in these data, including discussing infidelity on the part of the victim, abusive behavior by the victim, the victim's use of drugs and/or alcohol, and failure by the victim to use the legal system to protect herself. For example, one article detailed how a woman was killed after rescinding a temporary restraining order. It read, "[the victim] filed for a temporary restraining order a few days later that would have prohibited him from coming near her or the children, but she withdrew the request at a Family Court hearing the following month." The implication here is that the victim would not have been killed if she had allowed the police to protect her. Another article unnecessarily discussed how a woman was killed while on an alcohol-fueled binge. It stated, "While in Kona, [the victim] was 'messed up ' partying..." continuing, "Deciding to go to Hilo for more partying, she arranged on Sunday night to go to a scenic point with friends where she would be picked up..." This account, while not exculpating the offender, makes the victim seem morally questionable, and thus, less deserving of sympathy.

While some articles focused on the victims' faults and foibles, some other articles, employed indirect victim blaming, focusing on mitigating characteristics of offenders (Taylor 2009). The two main ways coverage indirectly blamed victims in this sample were characterizing the crime as sudden and inexplicable or by discussing how the offender suffered from intense stress (e.g. financial issues) or psychological illness. For example, one article read, "'I don't know what set the husband off,' [a neighbor] said. 'He seemed so cordial, always saying, 'Hi'. I guess sometimes things get so hard you don't know how to deal with it.'" This discourse at least partially exculpates the offender, ascribing the crime to extraordinary and inexplicable conditions. On the other hand, many articles excused the offender by citing mental illness, a bitter custody battle, or extreme financial strain, a finding which mirrors previous research (Gillespie et al. 2013; Taylor 2009). For example, one article avoided characterizing the crime as domestic violence, instead ascribing his crime to mental illness, stating, "Psychiatrist Edward Furukawa, one of three court-appointed mental health experts, found that Lam was under a delusion that the devil was in his wife when he struck her." Surely some perpetrators do suffer severe mental illness, and some femicides may be unexpected to neighbors and even family. Yet, focusing on such elements constructs these crimes as largely unpreventable or aberrant incidents, rather than domestic violence. Thus, since these incidents are not part of a broad social problem, they are framed as unfortunate but ultimately unpreventable.

SYMPATHY-BUILDING COMPONENTS

Though many blamed victims, some articles built sympathy for victims, for example by discussing children left motherless, family grief, the potential of the victim's life, and/or temporary restraining orders (TROs). This sympathy building was foundational construction material for the social problem frame.

Fourteen stories were commendable in that they provided sympathetic accounts of victims' lives. I call such accounts sympathy narratives. These stories discussed histories of abuse, stories of survival, obstacles faced by battered women, and victim achievements. For example, one article read,

> [The victim], 26, fell into an abusive relationship compounded by 'ice,' or crystal methamphetamine, after she met [the offender]... [the victim] overcame her own habit just a few months ago without professional help, Ryan said....

'She had family,' Ryan said. 'She hit rock bottom, then totally changed her life around....'

> [the victim] kept a hand written list of her goals in her wallet, often showing it to friends and family. She wanted to save money, take care of her baby and 8-year-old daughter from a previous marriage, and maybe buy a business one day."

By associating her drug abuse with her attacker and lauding her accomplishments and goals, this article constructs a redemptive, sympathetic victim. This coverage is clearly superior to that which blames the victim or fails to problematize domestic violence.

Another way articles built sympathy for victims was through discussion of TROs, a fact noted by Bullock and Cubert's (2002) study. About 15.5 % of articles (N=19) discussed TROs, often prominently. These articles often identified the crime as domestic violence, and used less forensic reporting. More broadly, they were sympathetic to victims, humanizing them and vilifying offenders by recounting a history of abuse and/or detailing the viciousness of abuse. For example, one article read,

> [The victim] filed for a temporary restraining order on March 10, alleging [the offender] repeatedly abused and threatened her.

> According to the court filing, [the victim] said [the offender] "refuses to accept the fact that our relationship is over" and that at one point he allegedly told her, "If I ever see you with another man, I will kill you with a sashimi knife."

> [The victim] said that [the offender] kicked, bit and raped her in January. In February, she said he punched and slapped her and stepped on her in an attempt to "crush my head with his foot."

This passage illuminates abuse by illustrating that femicides are often not spontaneous, but are part of a pattern of escalating violence. Furthermore, it humanizes the victim through her own words. This clearly diverts from forensic coverage that merely regurgitates mundane details such as victim/offender names, crime location, etc.

Sympathy narratives are surely superior to simplistic or victim-blaming coverage. However, they are not entirely unproblematic. Sympathy narratives are often contingent on particular forms of victim agency, for example, attempting to leave an abuser. This might encourage blaming victims who are unable to attempt leaving an abuser. Additionally, emphasizing TROs without discussing structural/cultural solutions implies that the criminal justice system is the only appropriate solution to domestic violence. Furthermore, articles tended to imply TROs were highly effective, portraying these femicides as the rare exceptions when TROs were not effective. Yet, research has shown that TROs are often ineffective in cases of severe abuse (Grau, Fagan, and Wexler 1984; Harrell and Smith 1996). Finally, one might argue that the emphasis on individual agency implicit in sympathy narratives is a masculinist standard that perpetuates patriarchy.

Essentially, these discourses conceal the role of patriarchy by suggesting that the state has already provided for women the tools with which to combat DV and that the responsibility of accessing these tools is ultimately up to victims. Still, coverage including sympathy narratives and TRO discussions was more contextualized and sympathetic than coverage employing the acceptable violence frame.

The preceding discussion of these eight story components— characterization as DV, official source use, alternative (family/friends or advocate/experts) source use, forensic reporting, ambiguous headlines, victim-blaming, sympathy narratives, and TRO discussions—illuminates the foundations of the divergent femicide framing in Hawaii news. Table 1 provides the frequencies of these components in the sample. Some of these components, such as forensic reporting, help to create a rather decontextualized, non-problematizing representation of femicides. I call this the acceptable violence frame. However, some components, such as identification of the crime as domestic violence, create an alternate representation of femicides that was far more sympathetic to victims—the social problem frame. As mentioned earlier, these themes constitute patriarchal discourse in that they selectively portray domestic violence, inhibiting public appreciation for this crime as a social problem and patriarchal product (Dragiewicz 2011; Howe 1997; Kozol 1995; Meyers 1994; Walby 1989; Websdale and Alvarez 1998). However, these two frames and their wider ideological role are more apparent when examined in a manner accounting for class-based and racializing discourses. The next section will discuss how class and race contribute to the disparate framing of femicides in Hawaii.

TABLE 1- KEY STORY COMPONENTS

Component	Frequency (%)
DV characterization	37 (30.3)
Official sources	119 (97.5)
Alternative sources	54 (44.3)
Forensic reporting	58 (47.5)
Ambiguous headline	87 (71.3)
Victim blaming	23 (18.9)
Sympathy narrative	14 (11.5)
TRO discussion	19 (15.6)

REPRESENTATIONS OF CLASS

Signifiers of class[3] were integral to frame construction in this sample. Specifically, lower class signifiers for victims and upper class signifiers for offenders tended to coincide with patriarchal discourse, while the obverse victim/offender permutations tended to co-occur with contextualization and sympathy narratives. This coincidence of class-based and patriarchal discourses further illuminates the disparate nature of the social problem and acceptable violence frames.

Table 2 compares the frequency of key story components' occurrence in lower class victim stories and that of middle or upper class victim stories. This sample contained 20 articles reporting on notably lower class victims and 49 featuring middle or upper class victims. Simplifying or decontextualizing story components were more common in lower class victim articles while contextualizing or sympathizing components were less common. These articles had a markedly higher occurrence of forensic reporting and victim blaming. Moreover, they had no-

---

[3] Class was coded for based on discussions of victims' and offenders' incomes, occupations, wealth (e.g. houses), and residences (e.g. reputedly wealthy or poor communities).

ticeably lower frequencies of DV characterization, alternative sources, and sympathy narratives. On the other hand, both categories of stories employed official sourcing, and TRO discussions in similar frequencies, while lower class victim stories featured fewer ambiguous headlines. However, it is important to note that official sourcing and ambiguous headlines were present in the vast majority of all articles. Overall though, these data demonstrate a pattern where signifiers of lower class status coincide with simplistic, blaming, or generally unsympathetic coverage. Conversely, signifiers of middle class standing coincide with contextualized and/or more sympathetic coverage.

TABLE 2- STORY COMPONENTS BY CLASS

Component	Lower-class Victims N=20 (%)	Middle-/Upper-class Victims N= 49 (%)
DV Characterization	5 (25.0)	21 (44.8)
Official Sources	20 (100.0)	48 (98.0)
Alternative sources	6 (30.0)	32 (65.3)
Forensic Reporting	11 (55.0)	16 (32.7)
Ambiguous headline	14 (70.0)	40 (81.6)
Victim blaming	7 (35.0)	9 (18.3)
Sympathy narrative	2 (10.0)	12 (24.5)
TRO discussion	4 (20.0)	10 (20.4)

Examining representations of offender class revealed several important patterns as well. This sample included 32 articles featuring lower-class offenders and 43 featuring middle or upper class offenders. Offender-based patterns were less clear than victim-based ones, because of the lack of cases featuring offenders and victims of different classes. Many articles constructed victim and offender class simultaneously, for example by stating that both lived in subsidized housing. Thus, disentangling victim and offender treatment is difficult. However, articles featuring middle or upper class offenders did tend to be more sympathetic to abusers. While constructing a picture of class, these articles often employed the indirect victim blaming tactics mentioned before, framing femicides as inexplicable tragedies or as a result of mental illness (Taylor 2009). For example, one article on a middle-class offender read,

> The [victim's family] recently purchased a home in the middle-, upper-income Waikoloa Village subdivision, and had bought a home for their oldest daughter, who lives only a block away.

It continues,

> [the pastor] of Solid Rock Ministries, which counted the [victim's family] among its 900 members, called the tragedy 'a total shock... something that wasn't expected.'

Another article, reporting on a murder-suicide, constructs a similar family portrait, reading,

> Stunned neighbors described the couple as friendly and happy, and the family as the least likely for such tragedy to ever befall. The question for almost all who have pondered the situation since, is, why? So far, there have been few answers."

It continues, describing the offender as the

> ...father of four children, now orphaned, [the victim's] high school sweetheart and life partner for two decades—and the person responsible for so much grief and sorrow for which there's *no logical explanation* [emphasis added].

Of course it would be inhumane to deny sympathy for anyone who takes his own life. However, excusing these offenders is still problematic because it prevents a holistic framing of domestic violence that captures the diversity of the crime. Moreover neither article problematizes the crime by truly implicating an offender. Instead they both construct a description of a tranquil middle-class family and a 'shocking' tragedy. One might say something similar about a family killed by a natural disaster. Nineteen of 43 middle or upper class offender articles described the crime as a mystifying tragedy or as a result of mental illness. On the other hand, only two articles with lower class offenders implicated mental illness while none described the crime as inexplicable. Thus, it seems class is intertwined with discourses building sympathy for offenders. Ultimately, this works to exclude middle and upper class offenders from the social problem frame.

To better disentangle class-based treatment of victims from that of offenders, I examined articles featuring victims and offenders of different classes. There were no articles featuring middle or upper class offenders and victims of a lower or unspecified class. However there were a limited number of articles featuring lower class offenders and victims of a higher or unspecified class. These articles were generally more contextualized and sympathetic to victims, while often vilifying offenders. Table 3 provides the frequencies of key story components for these articles.

TABLE 3- LOWER CLASS OFFENDERS AND MIDDLE OR
UNSPECIFIED CLASS VICTIMS

Component	Frequency (%) N=15
DV characterization	10 (66.7)
Official sourcing	15 (100.0)
Alternative sourcing	9 (60.0)
Forensic reporting	4 (26.7)
Ambiguous headline	7 (58.3)
Victim blaming	2 (16.7)
Sympathy narrative	6 (50.0)
TRO discussion	7 (58.3)

Compared to the wider sample, these articles far more frequently characterized the crime as DV, employed alternative sources, and included sympathy narratives or TRO discussions. Additionally, they less frequently engaged in forensic reporting or victim blaming and used fewer ambiguous headlines. However, theses articles did rely on official sources slightly more than the wider sample. Perhaps most important though, half of these articles employed powerful sympathy narratives that framed the victim as an innocent, productive member of society, victimized by an intimate who wouldn't let her go unless she was dead. For example with a headline reading, "She Was Turning Her Life Around" one article began,

[The victim], a mother of five, was turning her life around, leaving a bad relationship, joining a church and reconciling with her husband, relatives said yesterday.

But the boyfriend she left behind with her old life had other ideas, first stalking her, then breaking into her car and finally hunting her down.

This juxtaposition of innocent victim with villainous offender constructs domestic violence as a crime against successful women victimized by underclass predators. These articles exemplify the social problem frame, giving the message that domestic violence is horrific and unacceptable. However, they seem contingent on victims meeting a rather high standard of sympathy.

The above discussion shows how each frame is constructed with the aid of disparate class-based discourses. Femicides tend to be problematized through discussions of upper-/middle-class victims and/or lower-class offenders. On the other hand, the murder of lower class women tends to be covered in the simplistic and unceremonious manner that I call the acceptable violence frame. Complementing this, the crimes of upper/middle-class men are characterized as somewhat excusable or completely inexplicable. The following discussion will show how racialized coverage plays a similar role in frame construction.

RACIALIZED PATTERNS

Because of the complexity of racial hierarchy in Hawaii, and its surrounding discourse, I found 'race' to be a poor analytical lens. Accounting only for racial identities, one might argue that Hawaii's newspaper coverage of femicides is more racially inclusive. For example, it might appear that coverage restrains from othering Asians. Instead, analyzing racializing discourses was far more useful, revealing several patterns, some stark, and some subtle[4]. Findings suggest that coverage in Hawaii sometimes shadows mainland media coverage, for example, by covering black offenders in a particularly criminalized manner. However, most patterns did not involve a white/non-white

---

[4] Coding for race and ethnicity was based on several indicators such as images, place of crime occurrence, and surname. However, only about half (N=66) of all articles were coded for race/ethnicity.

schema that might be employed in mainland coverage. Various markers other than overt race, such as ethnicity, immigration status, and nationality, formed patterns that suggested racialized coverage. These themes coincided with the above-discussed patriarchal discourses, adding complexity to the disparate framing of femicides in Hawaii.

Despite Hawaii's diverse ethnic composition, my findings suggest that Hawaii's newspapers construct young black men in the same discriminatory criminal light as mainland media do (Chiricos and Eschholz 2002). There were a tiny number of black offenders in this sample—eight articles, featuring only three offenders. However, these few articles displayed an interesting phenomenon; six of these articles displayed the mug shot of the offender juxtaposed with the image of the white female victim right next to it. Only eight other articles (all featuring non-white offenders) did this. The positioning of a scowling black offender's photo right next to one of a smiling, innocent-looking, white female framed the crime as heinous black on white sexual violence, feeding into pervasive, fear-mongering stereotypes regarding black men, crime, and sex (Kozol 1995). Making any claims about bias in reporting would be inappropriate given the small amount of data relating to this pattern. However, the pattern in this limited data is very suggestive. It appears that, even in Hawaii, young black offenders lie at the bottom of a racialized hierarchy of coverage.

Foreign citizens and/or recent immigrants also seemed to be the subjects of racializing coverage. Articles frequently mentioned an immigrant or foreigner's status. Conversely, no articles describing native-born American offenders or victims mentioned their citizenship status. One article, describing the murder of a bartender by her former boyfriend, read, "Police records show that Park, a native of South Korea, was arrested for harassment in 2001 and twice for abuse in 2000..." Though such a detail is something a trained reporter would likely note and report, it is not really relevant to the crime. The inclusion of this detail comes at the expense of more relevant information— an identification of the crime as domestic violence for example.

Other articles went beyond merely mentioning superfluous details about immigrant/foreigners, providing unsympathetic, or one might even argue harsh, coverage toward immigrant victims. One article, describing the murder of a Singaporean woman and her mother by a Navy man, directly blamed the victim. It read,

> ...[the offender], charged with murdering his second wife and her mother, couldn't seek a divorce from her because he feared losing custody of his three children, his first wife said at a Navy hearing.

The article continues,

> [the offender's first wife] said [the offender] believed that his Singapore-born wife was seeing sailors whom she met at a Pearl Harbor 'single sailors' bar,' where she worked as a waitress.

Coverage discussing this woman's supposed infidelity and a custody battle hints that the victim's behavior was a contributing factor to her murder (Meyers 1994; Taylor 2009). Other articles went as far as to suggest the victim in this case was attempting to take the offender's children away to Singapore, again framing the victim as an adulteress ready to steal her husband's children away to a foreign country. In fact, this article was one of several articles from the sample that covered this murder. Other articles exhibited similar themes. For example, one described the victim as a "foreigner who loved to travel" who "met her husband to be in the United States," suggesting some sort of 'green card' marriage. Though this sample contained relatively few immigrant/foreigner victims or offenders, the articles present exhibited a pattern of less sympathetic, often victim-blaming, coverage and unnecessary 'outing' of their immigrant status.

Immigrant status is not an ethnicity per se. However, it is highly relevant to identity in Hawaii, especially considering Okamura's (1992) arguments about the pan-ethnic 'local' identity. Recent immigrants from Asia may be seen as outsiders by 'locals' who themselves have some Asian heritage, but downplay it in favor of the local identity. Ultimately, discussion of immigration status works as a racializing marker, helping to frame foreigners as an out-group.

Several of the immigrants outed in coverage came from the Philippines. Filipinos are a somewhat stigmatized group in Hawaii, associated with lower class status and domestic violence (Okamura 2008). Given this, Filipino/a victims and offenders were unsurprisingly featured prominently in many articles. Twenty-eight articles featured Filipina victims, while 29 articles featured Filipino offenders. Given their stigmatization, we might expect Filipina victims to receive less favorable coverage. In some ways, the sample confirms such a hypothesis. However, in other ways it does not. Table 4 compares the frequencies for key story components in articles featuring Filipina victims to those for stories featuring non-Filipina victims.

TABLE 4- FILIPINA VICTIMS

Component	Filipina Victims N=29 (%)	Non-Filipina Victims N= 94 (%)
DV characterization	6 (21.4)	31 (33.0)
Official sources	28 (100.0)	91 (96.8)
Alternative sources	14 (50.0)	40 (42.6)
Forensic reporting	13 (46.4)	45 (47.9)
Ambiguous headline	17 (60.7)	70 (74.5)
Victim blaming	8 (28.6)	15 (16.0)
Sympathy narrative	1 (3.6)	13 (13.8)
TRO	6 (21.4)	13 (13.8)

Table 4 shows that Filipina victim articles less frequently characterized femicides as DV, and more frequently employed victim blaming. On the other hand, these articles more frequently used alternative sources and discussed TROs, while they less frequently featured ambiguous headlines. Additionally, there were only minor differences in the use of official sources and forensic reporting. However, perhaps the clearest distinction between these two types of articles was their use of sympathy narratives. Only one article featuring a Filipina victim employed a sympathy narrative. Thus, it seems there is a subtle pattern in which Filipina victims tend to be framed with the acceptable violence frame.

The above-mentioned pattern is subtle rather than stark. However, when examining Filipina identity and class simultaneously, a clearer distinction emerges. The tendency to place Filipina victims in the acceptable violence frame was more extreme in articles covering lower-class Filipina victims. Table 5 compares the frequencies of key story components for lower class Filipina victim articles to those for middle class Filipina victim articles.

TABLE 5- FILIPINA VICTIMS ACCOUNTING FOR CLASS

Component	Lower Class N=7 (%)	Middle Class N=6 (%)
DV characterization	0 (0.0)	4 (66.6)
Official sources	7 (100.0)	6 (100.0)
Alternative sources	1 (14.3)	6 (100.0)
Forensic reporting	3 (42.9)	0 (0.0)
Ambiguous headline	4 (57.1)	5 (83.3)
Victim blaming	4 (57.1)	0 (0.0)
Sympathy narrative	0 (0.0)	1 (16.7)
TRO discussion	0 (0.0)	1 (16.7)

Compared to those featuring middle class Filipina victims, articles featuring lower class Filipina victims featured more victim blaming and forensic reporting, while they featured less DV characterization, fewer alternative sources, sympathy narratives, and TRO discussions. However, lower class articles did more frequently employ ambiguous headlines. Still the pattern is clear, it is not just Filipina victims who are covered differentially, but more so, lower class Filipina victims.

These findings suggest that coverage stigmatizes the Filipino/a identity somewhat (especially for lower-class individuals). Though Filipinos might be considered racially Asian (or

Latino), in this coverage, they occupy a specific ethnic space, which is subordinated in Hawaii's racialized hierarchy. This, and other markers (blackness, immigration status, nationality) suggest that though Hawaii newspaper coverage does not construct a white/non-white binary, it still relies on racialized themes to frame femicides. Furthermore, these racialized themes are material for the social problem and acceptable violence frames. Stigmatizing racialization helps to form the acceptable violence frame, while the absence of it helps to locate a crime within the social problem frame.

DISPARATE FRAMES REVEALED

The above-discussed findings illustrate how Hawaii's newspapers frame femicides disparately, as a social problem, or as unproblematized, generic crime. I call these characterizations the 'social problem' frame and the 'acceptable violence' frame, respectively. These data show that the frames are founded upon patriarchal ideas, such as conceiving of femicides as different from domestic violence. Yet, they are also constructed with classist and racialized discourses. Because these three types of discourses intersect in the social problem and acceptable violence frames, coverage constitutes a hegemonic ideology that perpetuates existing hierarchies built simultaneously upon race, class, *and* gender distinctions.

The social problem frame constitutes improving, yet still flawed, reporting. It problematizes femicides by acknowledging that they are domestic violence (contextualization); cultivating sympathy for the victim; characterizing the offender as the sole culpable party, or even predatory counterpart to victim-as-heroine; implying the victim is an economically productive member of society; and locating the victim in the racial/ethnic in-group through the omission of racialized themes. The social problem frame implies that femicide is unacceptable, that it is a serious issue, which society must address. It even hints that we have taken strides in solving the problem (e.g. TROs). However, it only selectively problematizes femicides.

The acceptable violence frame, on the other hand, demonstrates the flaws in coverage that scholars have critiqued for decades. This frame is built upon a routinized and neutral reporting mode, which communicates neither the significance of femicides, nor their patriarchal roots (Websdale and Alvarez 1998). This frame is largely a frame of omission; it is marked mostly for what is left out, not what is included. The acceptable violence frame fails to acknowledge femicides as domestic violence and dehumanizes the victim. Instead of contextualizing the crime, or illustrating the victim's suffering, this coverage focuses on minute details that tell the reader much about little. Often, the victim is characterized as lower class. Moreover, this frame may even hint that the victim was a culpable party, by using euphemisms, such as 'domestic dispute' to explain the crime. In some, less common, cases, the acceptable violence frame may imply that the crime was unavoidable, a product of extreme or mysterious circumstances. In such cases, though copious coverage may be given, reporting implies the crime could not be anticipated. Thus, it is not constructed as a documented, patterned, and pervasive phenomenon (domestic violence), which society must address. Ultimately, the acceptable violence frame characterizes femicides as either routine products of a problematic underclass, or mysterious tragedies suffered by middle and upper class families; neither of which can be systematically addressed by society, and therefore, must be *accepted*.

Finally, these two frames are ideal-typical, analytical tools, not empirical phenomena. No articles exhibited all the elements of one frame. Some articles blended the properties of both frames. I do not argue that there are two singularly employed manners of reporting on femicides in Hawaii. Instead, articles use two disparate narrative sets—one, which problematizes femicides, another, which ignores, excuses, or mystifies them. These two narrative sets might be used in the same article, but there is most often a preponderance of one, outweighing the other to form a specific frame. More often than not, the narrative set that problematizes femicides, the social problem frame, is absent. Instead coverage uses the acceptable violence frame, making these crimes seem somewhat routine, unproblematic, or inevitable.

CONCLUSION

Coverage of femicides in Hawaii somewhat shadows coverage analyzed in earlier studies. Basically, news still does a poor job of identifying femicides as domestic violence (Gillespie et al. 2013). Also, coverage fails to communicate that VAW is a widespread phenomenon, which springs from, and supports, patriarchy (Howe 1997). Yet, some coverage does acknowledge domestic violence, but, mostly when suffered by some women, and/or perpetrated by some men (Dragiewicz 2011). This constitutes disparate framing—the suffering and crimes of some are condemned, while those of others are ignored or mystified. Essentially, these findings illustrate limited evolution from the press' former ignorance of domestic violence. Instead of telling one story, this coverage tells two stories—that of a social problem and that of acceptable violence.

Many previous studies focusing specifically on victim-blaming or other patriarchal discourses have made important contributions (see Gillespie et al. 2013; Richards, Gillespie, and Smith 2011; Taylor 2009). However, more research is needed that also accounts for class and race. This study helps to do that by examining femicides with an intersectional orientation. Though of limited generalizability, this study also furthers VAW media research by refining understandings of victim and offender constructions and the mode of racialization in hegemonic ideology.

The identification of the disparate social problem and acceptable violence frames illuminates not just flaws in coverage, but also how the press constructs worthy and unworthy victims, sympathetic and unsympathetic offenders (DeKeseredy 2010; Dragiewicz 2011). These disparate frames allow us to better understand selective femicide coverage. It is not that the press merely ignores, or under-reports femicides. It is that reporting constructs femicides as a social problem when suffered or perpetrated by only selective, hegemonically convenient groups. Other femicides are constructed in a far less condemnatory and informative manner.

Furthermore, this analysis might help us better understand how femicide coverage works as intersectional hegemonic ideology. As Meyers (1994) states, femicide coverage does not simply obscure these crimes, it performs a hegemonic function by concealing wider power structures, of which VAW is a product. Analysis of hegemonic discourse in Hawaii has some unique implications. One might argue that coverage in Hawaii's newspapers illuminates the supporting discourse for a localized hegemony (Connell and Messerschmidt 2005), most distinctive in regards to race.

As mentioned earlier, I did not investigate *race*, but *racializing discourse*. When investigating racialization, nuanced othering is apparent—reporting employed several racializing markers (e.g. blackness, immigration status, Filipina identity) as part of the acceptable violence frame. Thus, we can see that Hawaii's newspapers do not merely use a white/non-white dichotomy, nor do they use an inclusive, de-racialized discourse. But, as part of their disparate framing, they employ nuanced and insidious racialized discourse, which, in the end, still perpetuates pre-existing hierarchies. Such insights might be generalizable to analysis of 'post-racial' discourse in mainland crime coverage.

One of the defining characteristics of hegemonic ideology is its capacity for evolution (Gitlin 2003; Hall et al. 1978). The social problem frame illustrates such flexibility, making it seem like society is acknowledging and addressing VAW. Conversely though, the acceptable violence frame naturalizes VAW by employing insidious patriarchal, classist, and racialized discourse. Ultimately, this coverage still creates an ideological schema that reflects and naturalizes existing hierarchies.

Domestic violence is clearly a significant social problem, linked, many would argue, to hegemonic conditions. We may only defeat this problem through cultural awareness and rejection of both. Media are an important vehicle for this. However, they cannot raise awareness without providing holistic and critical accounts of domestic violence. Yet, it seems at this point, they continue to give only facile analysis, which supports dominant ideas about the naturalness and inevitability of existing power structures—they continue to paint inequality as justice.

APPENDIX 1: SAMPLE CODE SHEET

Field	Description
Article ID#	
DATE	Article date
PUB	Publication
HEAD	Headline
#WRDS	Number of words?
modedeath	How did the victim die?
Weapn	Weapons used?
crimloc	Location of crime?
alcohol	Was alcohol present?
alcinvolvement	Was alcohol used?
alcstring	Notes on alcohol?
drugs	Where drugs present?
druginvolvement	Were drugs used?
drgstring	Notes on drugs?
sources	Primary source cited.
crimdetail	Crime details included?
m/s?	Was the crime a murder-suicide?
history	Describe the relationship history
motive	What was the crime motive?
expcrime	How was the crime explained?
vicrolestring	What role did the victim play?
victimblame	Is victim blaming present?
raceoff	Race of offender
racestring	Notes on race?
offenderplace	Where did they offender live?
imm/foroff	Was the offender an immigrant?
natoff	Nationality of offender
offfil	Was the offender Filipino?
offclass	Offender class
classtring	Notes on class
dvdisc	Was domestic violence discussed?
dvdiscussion	crimetrendstring
memo	
amibighead	Was there an ambiguous headline?
other notes	Other notes?
forensic reporting	Is forensic reporting employed?
TRO	Are TROs discussed?

vicname	Victim name.
V/O relationship	What was the victim/offender relationship?
vicrace	Victim race
vicnat	Victim nationality
vicimm/for	Was the victim an immigrant?
vicclass	Victim class
vicplace	Where did the victim live?
vicfil	Was the victim Filipina?
source1	First source cited
source 2	Second source cited
source 3	Third source cited

REFERENCES

Benedict, Helen. 1993. *Virgin Or Vamp: How the Press Covers Sex Crimes.* Oxford University Press.

Best, Joel. 1990. *Threatened Children: Rhetoric and Concern about Child-Victims.* University Of Chicago Press.

Bullock, Cathy Ferrand, and Jason Cubert. 2002. "Coverage of Domestic Violence Fatalities by Newspapers in Washington State." *Journal of Interpersonal Violence* 17(5): 475–99.

Burgess-Proctor, Amanda. 2006. "Intersections of Race, Class, Gender, and Crime: Future Directions for Feminist Criminology." *Feminist Criminology* 1(1): 27–47.

Chancer, Lynn. 1994. "Gender, Class and Race in Three High Profile Crimes: The Cases of New Bedford, Central Park and Bensonhurst." *Journal of Crime and Justice* 17(2): 167–87.

Charmaz, Kathy. 2006. *Constructing Grounded Theory: A Practical Guide through Qualitative Analysis.* 1st ed. Thousand Oaks, CA: SAGE Publications Ltd.

Chiricos, Ted, and Sarah Eschholz. 2002. "The Racial and Ethnic Typification of Crime and The Criminal Typification of Race and Ethnicity in Local Television News." *Journal of Research in Crime and Delinquency* 39(4): 400–420.

Connell, R. W., and James W. Messerschmidt. 2005. "Hegemonic Masculinity Rethinking the Concept." *Gender & Society* 19(6): 829–59.

DeKeseredy, Walter S. 2010. "Moral Panics, Violence, and the Policing of Girls." In *Fighting for Girls: New Perspectives on Gender and Violence*, eds. Meda Chesney-Lind and Nikki Jones. SUNY Press, 241–52.

Dragiewicz, Molly. 2011. *Equality With a Vengeance: Men's Rights Groups, Battered Women, and Antifeminist Backlash*. UPNE.

Gillespie, Lane Kirkland, Tara N. Richards, Eugena M. Givens, and M. Dwayne Smith. 2013. "Framing Deadly Domestic Violence Why the Media's Spin Matters in Newspaper Coverage of Femicide." *Violence Against Women* 19(2): 222–45.

Gilliam, Franklin D., and Shanto Iyengar. 2000. "Prime Suspects: The Influence of Local Television News on the Viewing Public." *American Journal of Political Science* 44(3): 560–73.

Gitlin, Todd. 2003. *The Whole World Is Watching: Mass Media in the Making and Unmaking of the New Left, With a New Preface*. 2nd ed. University of California Press.

Glaser, Barney, and Anselm Strauss. 1967. *The Discovery of Grounded Theory: Strategies for Qualitative Research*. Aldine Transaction.

Gramsci, Antonio. 1971. *Selections from the Prison Notebooks*. eds. Quintin Hoare and Geoffrey Nowell Smith. International Publishers Co.

Grau, Janice, Jeffrey Fagan, and Sandra Wexler. 1984. "Restraining Orders for Battered Women." *Women & Politics* 4(3): 13–28.

Grover, Chris, and Keith Soothill. 1996. "'A Murderous 'underclass'? The Press Reporting of Sexually Motivated Murder." *The Sociological Review* 44(3): 399–415.

Hall, Stuart, Chas Critcher, Tony Jefferson, John N. Clarke, and Brian Roberts. 1978. *Policing the Crisis: Mugging, the State and Law and Order*. 1st Ed. Palgrave Macmillan.

Harrell, A., and B. Smith. 1996. "Effects of Restraining Orders on Domestic Violence Victims." *Do arrests and restraining orders work*: 214–42.

Henley, N. M., M. Miller, and J. A. Beazley. 1995. "Syntax, Semantics, and Sexual Violence Agency and the Passive Voice." *Journal of Language and Social Psychology* 14(1-2): 60–84.

Herman, Edward S., and Noam Chomsky. 2002. *Manufacturing Consent: The Political Economy of the Mass Media*. Pantheon.

Howe, Adrian. 1997. "'The War Against Women' Media Representations of Men's Violence Against Women in Australia." *Violence Against Women* 3(1): 59–75.

Jewkes, Yvonne. 2010. *Media & Crime*. Second Edition. SAGE Publications Ltd.

Kline, Sidney. 2010. *Statistics on Domestic Violence Homicides in Hawai'i*. Honolulu, HI: State Coalition Against Domestic Violence.

Kozol, W. 1995. "Fracturing Domesticity: Media, Nationalism, and the Question of Feminist Influence." *Signs* 20(3): 646–67.

Lundman, Richard J. 2003. "The Newsworthiness and Selection Bias in News About Murder: Comparative and Relative Effects of Novelty and Race

and Gender Typifications on Newspaper Coverage of Homicide."
Sociological Forum 18(3): 357–86.

Mason, Paul. 2006. "Lies, Distortion and What Doesn't Work: Monitoring
Prison Stories in the British Media." *Crime, Media, Culture* 2(3): 251–67.

McDonald, M. G. 1999. "Unnecessary Roughness: Gender and Racial Politics
in Domestic Violence Media Events." *Sociology of Sport Journal* 16:
111–33.

McMullan, John L. 2006. "News, Truth, and the Recognition of Corporate
Crime." *Canadian Journal of Criminology and Criminal Justice/La
Revue canadienne de criminologie et de justice pénale* 48(6): 905–39.

Meyers, Marian. 1994. "News of Battering." *Journal of Communication*
44(2): 47–63.

Ogle, Robbin, and Candice Batton. 2009. "Revisiting Patriarchy: Its
Conceptualization and Operationalization in Criminology." *Critical
Criminology* 17(3): 159–82.

Okamura, Jonathan Y. 1992. "Why There Are No Asian Americans in
Hawai'i: The Continuing Significance of Local Identity." In *Social
Process in Hawaii: A Reader*, ed. Peter Manicas. New York: McGraw-
Hill, 243–56.

———. 2008. *Ethnicity and Inequality in Hawai'i*. Temple University Press.

Richards, Tara N., Lane Kirkland Gillespie, and M. Dwayne Smith. 2011.
"Exploring News Coverage of Femicide: Does Reporting the News Add
Insult to Injury?" *Feminist Criminology* 6(3): 178–202.

Rohrer, Judy. 2008. "Disrupting the 'melting Pot': Racial Discourse in
Hawai'i and the Naturalization of Haole." *Ethnic and Racial Studies*
31(6): 1110–25.

Ryan, Charlotte, Mike Anastario, and Alfredo DaCunha. 2006. "Changing
Coverage of Domestic Violence Murders A Longitudinal Experiment in
Participatory Communication." *Journal of Interpersonal Violence* 21(2):
209–28.

Sacco, Vincent F. 1995. "Media Constructions of Crime." *The ANNALS of the
American Academy of Political and Social Science* 539(1): 141–54.

Schwartz, Martin D., and Walter S. DeKeseredy. 1993. "The Return of the
'Battered Husband Syndrome' through the Typification of Women as
Violent." *Crime, Law and Social Change* 20(3): 249–65.

Silent Witness. 2006. "States Results 2003."
http://www.silentwitness.net/states/us_map.htm.

Sorensen, C. A., B. Wood, and E. W. Prince. 2003. "Race and Ethnicity Data:
Developing a Common Language for Public Health Surveillance in
Hawaii." *Californian Journal of Health Promotion* 1(spec): 91–104.

Stanko, E. A. 2000. "Women, Danger, and Criminology." *Women, Crime,
and Justice: Contemporary Perspectives*: 13–26.

Surette, Ray. 2007. *Media, Crime, and Criminal Justice: Images, Realities and Policies*. 3rd ed. Wadsworth Publishing.

Taylor, Rae. 2009. "Slain and Slandered A Content Analysis of the Portrayal of Femicide in Crime News." *Homicide Studies* 13(1): 21–49.

U.S. Census Bureau. 2006. *State Rankings--Statisical Abstract of the United States: Violent Crimes per 100,00 Population--2006*. Washington DC.

———. 2010. *Hawaii Quick Facts from the U.S. Census Bureau*. Washington DC. http://quickfacts.census.gov/qfd/states/15000.html.

U.S. Department of Justice. 2010. *Crime in the United States, 2010: Uniform Crime Reports Expanded Homicide Data*. Washington DC. http://www.fbi.gov/about-us/cjis/ucr/crime-in-the-u.s/2010/crime-in-the-u.s.-2010/offenses-known-to-law-enforcement/expanded/expandhomicidemain.

Walby, Sylvia. 1989. "Theorising Patriarchy." *Sociology* 23(2): 213–34.

Websdale, Neil, and Alexander Alvarez. 1998. "Forensic Journalism as Patriarchal Ideology." In *Popular Culture, Crime, and Justice*, eds. Frankie Y. Bailey and Donna C. Hale. Belmont, CA: Wadsworth Publishing, 123–41.

Ivar Kreuger: An International Swindler of Magnitude

TAGE ALALEHTO

One of the most held securities in Western Europe during the 1920s were the securities of Kreuger & Toll Inc. (a Swedish match conglomerate). The company was headed by Ivar Kreuger, known as the "Match King". His business operation is a story of great success from 1910 to the fall of his business empire in 1932, when it became clear that Kreuger & Toll Inc., operated by Kreuger himself, had been a company built on falsified accounts, forged documents and concealed misappropriation of funds of a massive scale. Kreuger has been described as one of the worst financial swindlers during the 20th century, with the epicenter at the Great Crash of 1929. It was a swindle that was described as Napoleonic in its size compared to the contemporary swindles of Samuel Insulls, Richard Whitney, and Clarence Hatry (Galbraith 2009). This case was discussed in the Paramalat fraud case in Italy in 2003–04, when the case against the company founder Calisto Tanzi was compared to the case of Kreuger (Kumar, Flesher, and Flesher 2007). Also, the case of Bernie Madoff was illustrated as an imitation of Kreuger, with Kreuger as "the original Bernard L. Madoff" (Partnoy 2010, 432). In fact, Kreuger constructed the financial instrument off-balance sheeting which together with credit rating and regulatory licenses were one of the reasons for the financial meltdown in 2008 and to which Madoff owes credit to when he created his gigantic Ponzi-scheme.

In this essay I will discuss the case of Ivar Kreuger and the financial world which he belonged. The setting for the Kreuger

47

case can, in several ways, serve as an ideal type of the spirit of capitalism.[1] For instance, his prime goal was profit-making and to attain the goal of a libertarian capitalist who bred the attitudes and personal qualities that defended the free market, and would help protect his private interests and the interests of the shareholders in the corporation (Braithwaite 1988). It is a description that serves as a topic for an investigation for a critical criminological point of view, especially with the aim of unmasking the criminality of powerful and wealthy white collar criminals (Tombs and Whyte 2003). This unmasking process is understood as an empirical investigation of the "higher immorality," referring to the moral insensitivity of blunt conscience among white collar criminals, where the only thing that matters is the amount of money, regardless how you earned it (Mills 1971; Simon 1999; Wozniak 2009).

During the 1920s Kreuger was the living symbol of the excesses of financial values and wealth. He was decorated with the Grand Cross of the Legion of Honor by the French Parliament, he received an Honorary Doctor of Business Administration degree at Syracuse University and he decorated the frontpage of *Time Magazine* on Thursday 24 October, 1929 (just four days before the Great Crash). Kreuger represented the progressive standard of the world capitalism. In more respectful circles he was known as the Savior of Europe and the financial wizard on Wall Street. He made profits when everyone else lost money in markets which were heavily affected by political divergences due to the World War I (Clikeman 2009). The impact of the Kreuger-group in the world economy was very large. 1925–1931, the securities of Kreuger & Toll were one of the world's most extensive, as well as being one of the 15 companies with the highest turnover in the New York stock market. For example, in 1929, the securities of Kreuger & Toll traded for $76 million out of the overall $335 million (22.68%) in the New York stock market (Eddy, 1937; Partnoy, 2010). In the

---

[1] Capitalism refers to an economic system were the means of production is under private ownership and the production is regulated by market forces. The State or cooperatives has a limited influence on production and the means of production. Capitalism is to its nature expansive, it assumes a constant increase in resources and production to function well. To do this capitalism demands a political system where freedom to manufacture and sell is extensive with few or none privileges by the State (Ingham, 2013).

Stockholm stock market the K&T securities stood for 64% of the market's turnover and had 25% of the aggregated stock market value. Kreuger's own total capital asset in 1929 was valued at $1.4 billion (including private fortune, ownership and/or direct control of multinational companies). This can be compared to the total capital asset of 4 billion dollars in the Swedish banking system at the time (Cederschöild 1937; Thunholm 2003).

Kreuger's ability to financially zigzag through the political battlefields stood out amongst the financial circles. He had made money by introducing concession loans in all 15 nations in exchange for a match monopoly (including 2 additional nations in practice) during the 20s, thereby controlling around 65 per cent of the match production in the world. Through concession loans he gave US capital the possibility to invest and make profit from the urgent need that many of the European Nations suffered in the aftermath of the World War I. Beyond these he also introduced new kinds of shares by differing A-shares (one share/one vote) toward a new form of B-shares (one share/000.1 vote) in England and Sweden. This gave US corporations the possibility to invest its capital in, for example, Swedish industry which was otherwise forbidden by the Swedish Company Act. He also introduced new kinds of shares called "Participating debentures" which was a mix of an obligation and a share (giving as an obligation it guaranteed a certain minimum interest and as a share it gave higher interest if the dividend exceeded the minimum interest) whose returns were derived from the returns of other private investors in the public market in US, Sweden and England. That is, a variant of a Ponzi-scheme. He also became known as the inventor of off-balance-sheeting[2], a financing technique that is still practiced in the market today. And lastly, he created the corporate group Swedish Match Company, Kreuger & Toll Inc and Dutch Kreuger & Toll, which had up to 400 subsidiary and sub-subsidiary companies, and had fantastic profit margins throughout

---

[2] Refers to a debt beside the company's balance sheet. The debt belongs to an individual client direct or in trust while the company serves as depository for the client's debt. However the company can use this off-balance debt when it search for a loan by showing up no liabilities in its balance sheets. Even if this is the case in reality for the company.

the 1920's with up to approximately 30% revenues for shareholders in Kreuger & Toll Inc. annually (Partnoy 2010; 2011).

During the Great Crash of 1929 Kreuger began to get into serious liquidity problems, chiefly because of the decrease of US capital flow into Europe (Lönnborg, Ögren, and Rafferty 2011). In order to distribute the huge amount of capital for the concession loans to several nations (e.g. France 971.25 million dollars, Germany 1 683.75 billion dollar, etc)[3], he was forced to get short-term loans from the banks. The banks then pressed him to get even more short-term loans on securities which successively decreased in their value during the financial circumstances of the time. During this time it is alleged that Kreuger manipulated the balance sheets, used double book-keeping and falsified the validity of his securities in his emission loan negotiations with the banks. Just one month after his suicide on March 12th, 1932 (stressed by his gigantic liquidity and solvency problems in the Kreuger-group), a commission of bankruptcy in Sweden started an investigation of the Kreuger-group, including an audit investigation by Price, Waterhouse & Coppers. The Price Waterhouse report (which was actually 57 partial reports) found that Kreuger had been one of the greatest swindlers ever seen in the financial world up to that day, and according to some later commentators, also up to this day (Flesher and Flesher 1986; Kumar, Flesher, and Flesher 2007; Partnoy 2011; Shaplen 1960).

The relevance of critical criminology

There are several reasons why an investigation of white collar criminals should be investigated by critical criminologists, not least from a policy perspective as in the case of Ivar Kreuger. The endeavor to increase the transparency of a single business or a financier's activity is also an argument for the democratization of corporations. Internal members and the external investor's need transparency of the corporation's financial standing. Hidden criminality by the powerful can affect the workers'

---

[3] The monetary value of the dollar was adjusted to reflect updated exchange rates for 2011 by the consumer price index, in accordance with the calculator: "The Annual Consumer Price Index for the United States, 1774-2011", collected November 6, 2012 at
http://www.measuringworth.com/datasets/uscpi/result.php.

job security and in the long-term the society's tax base will harm the general contributions toward the most vulnerable people (DeKeseredy and Perry 2006).

A second kind of policy argument would be to strengthen the position of social categories at the lowest strata, arguing for the criminalization of white collar criminals in order to achieve general justice and reduce social harm by breaking the protection of special economic and political interests through strengthening the efficiency of regulatory agents and law enforcement toward white collar crime. Otherwise, white collar criminality can further deepen the inequalities in society because white collar crime mainly strike at the first-hand social categories (women, elderly, children, etc), and not individuals, as most street criminals do (Snider 2000; Alvesalo and Tombs 2002; Alvesalo, Tombs, Virta, and Whyte 2006; Slapper and Tombs 1999).

Regarding both of these policy issues, the case of Ivar Kreuger is a good example of what can happen in the absence of corporate transparency, when a company is led by a charismatic and autocratic leader, within an environment with weak regulations of accountancy, board members or law enforcement. As a consequence, there were many individual and organizational victims.

A methodological argument for a critical criminologist to choose a case such as Ivar Kreuger is given by David Friedrichs (2004). He suggested that critical criminologists should collect data on a corporate scandal systematically by applying an integrated theory approach in criminology where data can be collected at individual, organizational and institutional levels (see also Tombs 2008; Lasslett 2010). Critical criminologist should also initiate systematic studies of cases through exploring available ethnographical data. This can be an advantage on a case that contains data collected over a period of time. This may include information given by journalists, found in memoirs, from researchers, etc, which represent the narratives and discourse for the phenomena (Lasslett 2010; Williams 2008). This is especially possible in the case of Ivar Kreuger who was, in contrast to the majority of white collar criminals, a visible criminal for public outcry and even moral panic.

The Organizational Guide and Data for the Essay

In criminological theory the search for the 'cause' of crime and criminality is a complex issue, and using an integrated approach on individual, organizational and institutional levels is proposed (e.g. Farrington 2008). The integrative approach searches for the 'cause' in a hierarchy of variables, including the crime scene and personality type of the criminals, and continues to search through the levels of organizational culture of institutionalized profit-making in the market combined with the reforms that regulate or de-regulate business through politics. The overall idea in this essay is to examine how the interaction of these three abstract levels underpinned Kreuger's actions during the period of 1910–1932. Focal points are Kreuger's personality traits and his social background as rather static variables, to the interconnections to dynamic variables such as organizational, market factors, etc (Laub and Sampson 2003; Piquero, Farrington, and Blumstein 2007). For example, this essay will examine how the direction of the business interests among several agents' rallied around Kreuger's autocratic leadership, and how this set of variables coheres (or are framed) with the institutional structure of the market, the business moral and politics. This approach is then applied in a kind of a narrative through qualitative person-based analysis (Laub and Sampson 2003). The theoretical framework consists of rather general and explorative critical criminological concepts such as unmasking the crimes of the powerful, criticizing the higher immorality of big business and the lack of transparency of business operations and the need to make corporations more democratic.

The data collection includes various literatures, including, in order of priority, academic publications such as theses and peer-reviewed articles, academic-related works, journal articles, and memoirs. The literature will explore different topics such as the institutional settings of the market, the personality traits of Kreuger and, especially, the structure of the Kreuger-group. The data contends a rather high volume of investigations and commentaries from a wide variety of scientific disciplines in order to discuss the phenomena of Ivar Kreuger. This data consists partly of first-hand information, such as personal accounts, and partly of second-hand data which was dependent on information from other sources, such as the psychological and social background. Kreuger himself did not ever write anything concerning his life or made any slightest commentary over his life. However, his brother Torsten Kreuger, and several authors sponsored by him, wrote many commentaries on Ivar which emphasized his innocence, honesty, and his significance as a great businessman, particularly for the Swedish business world. Most of the later literature about him is biased by nationalism or is conspiracy-driven, such as alleging that members of the bankruptcy commission acted in its own interest and hid their own white collar criminality when accusing Ivar Kreuger of being a swindler. Nevertheless, I have chosen not to refer this literature as data due to its highly biased and speculative character.

THE INSTITUTIONAL AND CONDITIONAL SETTING OF THE MARKET DURING THE 1910s AND 20s

The environmental character of capitalistic Sweden during the first two decades of the 20th century was characterized as an age of optimism full of visions and grand plans for the future. A lot of industrial and financial projects were initiated and executed by commercial banks as intermediary agents conducting a speculative boom in the stock market (Lindgren 1982).

Kreuger wholly identified with this spirit and used his big business solutions, such as big mergers and big cartels, as the successful model for capitalistic entrepreneurship. He promoted these ideas to potential investors with his confidence and trustworthy attitude. By 1908 he, along with Paul Toll, had already started a successful construction company. They received several prestigious construction projects in Sweden, including Stockholm stadium, Blå Hallen in Stockholm city hall, and the department store of Nordiska Kompaniet in Stockholm. They also worked in Finland and Russia, which were Sweden's biggest export market before 1917 (Lönnborg, Ögren, and Rafferty 2011). Nearly every one of the contracts was profitable and Kreuger became increasingly respected in European business circles. By becoming a business celebrity he could expand his business contacts continuously and change his direction from engineering to financial business. In 1917 he created the holding company Kreuger & Toll (K&T). During the period 1917–

1924 K&T declared an exceptional profit level of 130.7 billion Skr[4], where Kreuger was personally in charge of 68 per cent of the profits (Thunholm 2003; Glete 1981).

As a parallel process to the process of building K&T, he also became an industrial capitalist of rank by creating The Swedish Match Inc. (STAB). He privately controlled 223,000 share units of the company's 450,000 total shares. From the very beginning, STAB showed good profit figures with 13.8 billion Skr in 1918 and up to 38.9 billion Skr in 1923. This was probably due to a lot of 'air' in the accounts by unnoticed accounting profits in STABs cash flow, at a period when the Swedish business world was generally not doing well (Thunholm 2003). As a consequence, in 1919, Kreuger was already one of the richest men in Scandinavia with a private fortune of 39 billion Skr (Shaplen 1960).

Like many other contemporaries in the market, Kreuger believed that the best way to make money was to control the market. Free enterprise in a free market was a means to control the market in order to form a monopoly and thereby increase the prices and the profits for the company. In the long-run capitalism would continuously expand the world economy and subsume more of the national markets under one international and coherent market system (Lindgren 1982).

At the start of the 1920s there was declining currency in Europe and rising demands for strong finances in order to meet the people's requests for social welfare. The people also wanted a strong military defensive position, economic growth through land reforms, and this bred a need for capital investment in most of the European nations. During these times politicians and financiers were in awe of Sweden's strong finances. Up to that time Sweden had been a small and quite insignificant financial agent in the world economy. Despite being in the periphery it had a good reputation in the business world because its banking system was well constituted although conservative and parochial in character.

---

[4] The monetary value of Swedish kroner was adjusted to updated exchange rates for 2006 by the consumer price index, in accordance with the list: "Consumer Price Index for Sweden 1291-2006" collected November 6, 2012 at http://www.riksbank.se/sv/Riksbanken/Forskning/Historisk-monetar-statistik/Priser/

Kreuger realized that the accumulated Swedish capital could bring benefit and pay interest to a more expansive finance politic, and turn Sweden into a significant financial agent in the world economy. Leading Swedish politicians and economists started to talk about the second period of the Swedish age of greatness. Kreuger started by borrowing money directly or by emissions from almost all banks in Sweden. This helped his expansion endeavor, first in the Swedish match industry by merging the highly divergent Swedish match industry under his control. Then he expanded into the Nordic match industry and finally in the European match industry through buying shares to get the control interests of the companies through a straw man. When the Swedish banking system became limited in capital assets for his expansion endeavor, he came into contact with the London office of Lee, Higginson & Co., who was at that time a leading investment bank. With their help he joined the American market in order to attempt in creating a match monopoly through transferring large amount of American capital to European nations (Soloveytchik 1933; Cederschöild 1937; Partnoy 2010).

Kreuger was trusted not only because of his successful entrepreneurial history and private fortune, but also his calm and confident attitude that made it seem as if there was no problem which couldn´t be solved. This attitude impressed most of the potential investors. Because of his personal capacities and the fact that he was successful in most of the emissions he promoted, many investors (small and large) came to invest in the large amount of emissions that he proclaimed during the 20s. The bulk of these emissions were financed by different kinds of shares and debentures, mainly participating and secured debentures. Most of the debentures were advertised in the USA (around 65%), then Sweden (around 15%), Switzerland (around 7%), and Great Britain (around 5%) (Glete 1981). In total 1,079.9 billion dollars[5] was transferred to Europe from 1923 to 1932 by the International Match Corporation (IMCO) (a Swedish-American holding company established by Kreuger and Lee, Higginson & Co. in 1923) through selling debentures,

---

[5] The monetary value was American CPI for 1959 converted to CPI for 2011 collected November 6, 2012 at
http://www.measuringworth.com/datasets/uscpi/result.php.

securities, and share units to the American public (Shaplen 1960). IMCO was, in practice, controlled by Kreuger through STAB, because STAB controlled more than 50% of IMCOs shares (Byttner 1951).

However, for Lee, Higginson & Co., Kreuger gave them the opportunity for successful investments in US capital. They trusted Kreuger as a channel into war-ravaged Europe, with his plans of match monopoly in the world which Lee, Higginson & Co could take advantage of (Hassbring 1979).

Kreuger's general idea from 1925 onward was to offer concession loans to nations with a desperate need for capital through his holding company (Kreuger & Toll Inc) in exchange for a monopoly contract of the match production for IMCO or directly for STAB (Shaplen 1960). Kreuger's strategy was to offer a loan with interest of 5–6%, where around half of the profit of the match sale was given to the government. In return, the contract demanded that STAB got a monopoly contract running for 25–30 years on all match production in the nation, where the government was obligated to secure that no other entrepreneur could produce, deliver or distribute matches over the contract period (Thunholm 2003). This was a win-to-win situation for Kreuger as well as for a short-sighted government policy. But for the match workers it meant mass-unemployment; for the consumers it meant the price of matches doubled. In the long run for the nation it meant the price of matches rose up to 2.5 times more than the cost of living (Wikander,1977).

THE SIGNIFICANCE OF PERSONALITY TRAITS

The political or social consequences of the monopoly contracts did not concern Kreuger. He was living up to the standards of a modern capitalist by conquering new markets, defeating competitors, and realizing his large projects with no other goal than to accumulate capital under his specific interests. According to the psychological analysis of Kreuger, he was a calm person, calculating, quiet and even shy; but extremely charismatic, highly intelligent, sophisticated and seemingly trustworthy. However, he had, at the same time, narcissistic traits including being emotionally distant, instrumentally engaged in his relationships and a lack of empathy for other people's feelings

(Bjerre 1932; see also Soloveytchik 1933; Cederschöild 1937). Ivar Kreuger was the third child in a siblings of six. His father Ernest August was the fifth generation of a family emigrated from Germany. Ernest August was the opposite of an intellectual, a conservative man with both feet on the ground working as a factory manager in Kalmar (a small city in south of Sweden). A position that did not impress on Ivar. His mother Jenny Kreuger, born in South Africa, was an unruly dominant housewife bearing on the mental illness that were in her family. Jenny and Ivar did not always get along, because Ivar was considered as mysterious and coy with his poker face. Ivar was regarded as the black sheep in the family (Partnoy 2011).

According to the Swedish psychoanalysts Poul Bjerre (1932), Kreuger was an amoral person. He could, for example, engage in dangerous activities, such as during his adolescence when he threw gunpowder straight into open fire just for fun. He could also do 'good' things, like when he tried to cheat in exams for the interest of a classmate, even without any advantage for himself. Above all, he was driven by a desire for experimentation and risk-taking. When attending school for engineering studies, his class had an exercise on calculations for a bridge. He 'borrowed' a plan from one classmate and the calculations from another and handed it over to the professor as his own work. He passed the exam.

Kreuger's amorality was due to his lack of empathy. He could not feel pain, either physical or mental, such as being homesick. Cognitively he had a quite an extraordinary capacity for problem-solving, and an excellent memory, but on the other hand he was emotionally very cold. He was driven by his clear, cold and incisive logic. He was also quick-witted. Kreuger could immerse himself with every small detail, yet his ability to judge other people was strictly limited. He could be careless when it came to domestic finances, but not when it concerned financial projects.

Overall, Kreuger was a rather uncomplicated person. He had no inhibitions questioning his grand plans. No kind of self-criticism, no soul-searching, just a passion to advance for his own recognition. In his ambition, everything could be exploited for the 'good' of his projects. His organizational skills were just below the standard, but his capacity to combine different aspects in order to find solutions to problems was exceptional. If he found an acceptable solution on a financial problem, which stood in conflict to the law, he explained laconically before his board of trustees: "It's not me doing the wrong thing, it's the law that's imperfect." (Bjerre 1932, 166; Cederschöild 1937).

Kreuger was also very good at fitting in with various communities. When he was in Sweden, he lived as a Swede; when he was in America, he lived as an American; when he was in France, he lived as a Frenchman. According to Cerderschöild (1937) this was an expression of Krueger's truly 'internationalism'. He did not like to identify himself as belonging to a specific nation. According to Bjerre, it is another example of Kreuger's absolute kind of isolated and opportunistic identity. He was capable of living comfortably in any context, without feeling any kind of psychological anguish. Another curiosity of Kreuger's character was the fact that he never got married, and so far as is known he had no serious plans to be married. According to rumors he had at least one mistress in most of the places in the world where he had an apartment: Stockholm, Berlin, Warsaw, Paris, and New York (Clikeman 2009). According to Cederschöild (1937) Kreuger was incapable of feeling love; he seemed to be distanced from his own feelings and what others felt for him.

All in all Kreuger showed some of the characteristics characterizing a psychopath as grandiose sense of self-worth, manipulative, lack of remorse or guilt and lack of empathy. To this we can probably add promiscuous sexual behavior and many short-term relationships (Babiak, Neumann, and Hare 2010)

THE KREUGER-GROUP

From the beginning of his construction engineering in 1908 with Paul Toll, Kreuger stipulated contracts which declared that if the building was delayed the construction company was forced to pay indemnity, but if the building was ready-built before the contract ran out the buyer had to pay a large bonus. In almost every construction project, they succeeded in completing the building before the contract ran out. They organized the labor force to work in such a way that the neighbors nearest to the building sites complained about the noise throughout the day.

Another characteristic of Kreuger's leadership was the division of control of the companies. Kreuger took care of all kinds of strategic, accounting and financial issues for the company in question, but he let the daily operational activities be run by his co-workers, which he trusted, even if they were not very gifted or even competent. One example from 1931 is when Kreuger was suspected, questioned and even informally accused by the banks and the state bank of deceitful accounting in the Kreuger-group. None of the board members or CEOs reacted openly with suspicion or resigned from the boards although some of them must have been aware, afterwards, that the accounts showed serious liquidity problems and cover-up operations in several of the companies in the group. Thereby the board members were signaling to the market, to potential investors and politicians (for example the Swedish Finance Minister F. Hamrin) that the Kreuger-group was solid (Trolle 1992).

In the Price, Waterhouse & Coopers reports Kreuger's co-workers were characterized as either unswervingly loyal to Kreuger or just weak-minded people (ref. by Shaplen 1960; Arlebäck 2000). Thereby, Kreugers dubious financial dealings could continue to save and keep up the business activities of the Kreuger-group by huge contributive loans from the Swedish banks through 1928–1930 (by around 256.3 billion skr, which was around 10% of the banks' total enfoldment) and from the Swedish State Bank in 1931 (around 396.75 billion skr equivalent with 2% of Swedish GDP 1931) until his suicide on March 12, 1932 (Gäfvert 1979). According to Gäfvert (1979) these huge contributive loans drained the Swedish business world of capital for other industrial investment opportunities. This weakened the financial position of the Swedish business world, forcing the Swedish government to abandon the gold standard in 1931 and caused political crises during the following years.

However, the board members of STAB, K&T and Dutch Kreuger & Toll and the CEOs in all the subsidiary companies and the accountants for each of the companies had little insight into the business maneuvers that Kreuger took in all issues concerning the Kreuger group as a unit. They also had no knowledge or insight into other parts of the Kreuger-group other than the company that they were responsible for. Kreuger kept the information short in front of his co-workers and demanded that every kind of business transactions had to be treated with secrecy and without any objections. He, therefore, controlled almost everything on his own (Arlebäck 2000; Partnoy 2010). When he made a decision he most often did it without any explanations, even for highly respected and experienced board members, such as Donald Durant, Percy Rockefeller, Fredric Allen at Lee, Higginson & Co. and Oscar Rydbeck at Skandinavbanken. In fact, this kind of secretive dealings around the companies and business operations was acknowledged, accepted and unquestioned as part of the business culture at the time (Glete 1981).

Kreuger took advantage of this business culture and treated all companies and subsidiary companies as one corporate group, despite the fact that they belonged to different industries, different countries and were ruled by different jurisdictions. In some cases this could exceed the legalities, for example, when the Swedish Skandinavbanken demanded a reinforcement of their securities to extend the credits for the Kreuger-group in 1931. In order to do this, Kreuger transferred a position of German obligations with the value of 738 million dollars, belonging to the German department of IMCO, without reporting it to the board of IMCO and without taking notice that it was listed on the stock exchange in the USA. Of the 738 million dollars he transferred 443.1 million to Skandinavbanken and kept 295.4 million as a reserve for prospective demands (Trolle 1992).

EXAMPLES OF KREUGER'S SWINDLES

Kreuger's general business strategy was to use off-balance-sheets. From 1910, he derived the profit goals at the start of a project in which the final accounts had to be adjusted in order to impress potential investors. If the project needed extra profit margins, he contributed through overtaking an unsure demand from other projects in the Kreuger-group. The largest financial risk by doing this was when the project resulted in a bonus allocation before it had been realized. To be successful this strategy was used on a permanent expansion. The rake-off for the current year was secured by the expectation of future profits for years to come (Glete 1981). In itself this was not an illegal strategy, but it was certainly a strategy that could lure one to act in an illegal manner if the conditions were right. In fact, there were plenty of "right" opportunities for manipulation. One of the most well-known examples was the systematic manipulations for the accounts of American Kreuger & Toll Inc. (AK&TI). AK&TI was constituted in 1919 and had a significant position in the accounting of Kreuger & Toll Inc. (the Holding company). Generally, there was a lack of information for the investors in what kind of business AK&TI was involved in, and were given no more than the general description that it was concerned with the capital export of American capital invested in the German real estate business. This was, in fact, true and this was a rather good capital investment, because the price of real estate did not increase at the same pace as the German currency decreased which meant that the value of real estate increased in relation to the decreasing currency.

Formally, the profit of this trade was noted in the AK&TI accounts, but its substantial profit was not distributed to the investors in AK&TI. Instead, it was funding the Holding company, thus strengthening the credit standing of the Holding company toward the banks and the private investors for the 30% required rate of return. To cover-up the profit figures in AK&TI in order to increase the credibility for emissions through AK&TI, Kreuger used different kinds of securities as STAB-shares (which it turned out were fakes) in order to establish the credibility for AK&TI. These and other similar kinds of emission-phonies were successful for Kreuger, and AK&TI was noted for a value of 6 million dollars. However, in reality its joint stock was not more than 500,000 dollars. The reason Kreuger could continue with these kinds of manipulations was due to the non-transparency for investors and the substantial lack of information over how large Kreuger's capital engagement was in the German real estate business. The investors and the regulatory agencies were referred to look only at the outcomes (Glete 1981).

A second example of his fraud was his selling of the telephone company L M Ericsson to the International Telephone & Telegraph Corporation for 11 million dollars, when the controller for Price Waterhouse discovered that "about 27.5 million Swedish crowns listed as 'cash' actually consisted of claims against Kreuger companies." (Wallerstedt 2001, 13). ITT wanted to cancel the contract and threatened to go to trial if he did not cancel the contract. After much pressure from ITT Kreuger chose to cancel the contract.

A third example of fraud was the annual fictitious income of 6 million dollars from Garanta (a Dutch subsidiary company in the Kreuger-group), which in reality did not operate any of the business at all. These three examples were, in fact, common examples of the way Kreuger controlled the accounts. He declared profits in the books, when in fact the profits had not yet been realized. He mortgaged and declared profits of the emissions as assets, without these having yet been realized and he mortgaged debts as assets to increase the credibility of the companies (Glete 1981). Much of these accounting operations were possible because, when Kreuger declared income and expenses in the books he used few, general and unspecified budget items which could mean practically anything (Gäfvert 1979).

Another way that Kreuger could continue to fraud the companies was through mixing up his own fortunes with the company's assets to finance a project. Quite often he'd sign a contract in his own name to hide the forthcoming affair from the competitors. After the contract had been officially declared he would transfer it to the interests of the actual company in the Kreuger-group, and reimburse his private expenses. The problem was that no one else actually knew how much money Kreuger spent signing the contract and how much money he reimbursed himself when the contract was officially declared.

An Explanation

Ivar Kreuger was, according to the literature, never sued over his lifetime. In the memoirs on him he is described as a gambler during his school years, prepared to take large risks against his and his acquaintances' best interests. Although a polished gambler when younger, his propensity for risk-taking became more grandiose over the years because of the financial resources he controlled. This preparedness to take risks was a static variable of Kreuger's. In fact, much of his eagerness in conquest can be explained as a static variable, even if the successfulness of the conquest must be understood in the context of dynamic variables interacting with the static variables. At least one source suggests that Kreuger started to manipulate the accounts by 1917, and he continuously made manipulations until his death in 1932 (Glete 1981). If this is true then Kreuger was a career criminal[6] for years, starting his criminal behavior at 37 years old and increasing his criminal activity up until his death at 52 years old.

Two other static variables of importance were Kreuger's amoral character and lack of empathy. In the psychological analysis of Kreuger, Bjerre gives evidence to describe him as anti-social. For instance, he lived without fear, and quite probably without guilt. He threw explosives into an open fire, bluffed his exams, showed no remorse for the consequences of his conquest plans, and expressing no soul-searching over the plans he made. Instead, he exhibited no feelings of fear or shame, just a calmness and restraint (or maybe better described as stoicism) as if there was nothing worth caring about. Cederschöild (1937) even described his social character as cynical. Through his attitude of "mind your own business" he could justify his criminal actions of falsified accounts (he had the right to do it), and in front of others he simply told nothing of the state of the companies' finances.

Other static variables when discussing his personality was his alienation from society and his opportunistic identity which allowed him to adjust to circumstances without showing any obvious psychological anguish, such as his ability to settle anywhere in the world. Instead he focused all of his attention on work and his aim to conquer and create a match monopoly across the globe through permanently negotiating loans, takeovers, offering emissions, debentures, etc. He was, in this sense, a true international businessman captured of the spirit of capitalism.

Linked to the above static variables is the fact that he had no children and was never married, which is identified as one basic protective factor toward criminality (Laub and Sampson 2003). By this, he simply had no one else to take care of, except the

---

[6] A carrier criminal is a person who have done at least four crimes or more during his life-time (Piquero, Farrington, & Blumstein, 2007:132-135).

rather superficial relationships with his mistresses and family in Kalmar (which he visited only at Christmas time). The only person he took care of, to some extent, was his youngest sister Britta, who visited him several times in Paris and London. Overall, he held, as far the literature tells it, a very discretionary attitude toward his family when discussing his business activities, even with his younger brother Torsten, who was known as a successful businessman in Sweden (Trolle 1992). He stood alone with his feelings, probably caused by his discretionary attitude (refusing intimacy) and his preoccupation with work. Thus, to him there was nothing else of equal importance to his work. This says something about Kreuger's history of employment (counted as another protective factor of significance toward criminality). Kreuger was never unemployed during his lifetime, which does not mean that he was a wealthy man from adolescence, but that he received a regular income from the labor market from an early age (Thunholm 2003).

Given the impact of these static variables and how they interact with the institutional setting at the time that Kreuger came into the business world, it is seen as a crucial link in explaining how Kreuger could progress his career. Obvious cultural factors such as the optimistic era of capitalism which encouraged entrepreneurship of all kinds were one factor of importance for the decade of 1910 to 1920. Another important cultural factor was the acceptance of monopolies in business, especially in the European nations. A third important factor was the acceptance of un-democratic business-dealing with accounting and hidden decision-making. A fourth important institutional factor was the political reconstitution of the European nations after World War I, where the demand for expensive social reforms required capital from the governments. Some of the requests were hard to meet because of the absence of capital in several European nations. When a request could be met, this created a fifth kind of institutional factor, by the rather well consolidated but limited Swedish banking system and by the US financial system which contended with an over-abundance of capital which wanted to be invested profitably somewhere.

All these institutional factors created an ideal setting for Kreuger. He was raised in an entrepreneurial family which held entrepreneurial values. He was encouraged by the markets to build a monopoly which suited his psychological fixation of conquering the world. Especially through the latter institutional setting he could perform as a hero through saving the world with his conquest, yet eagerly at the same time guaranteeing high profits for the Krueger-group and high revenues for investors.

An example of higher immorality could be shown when the expectation of business, given by Lee, Higginson & Co., was a claim that everything "that worked" was "good business", especially such business that avoided taxes and met a required rate of return of around 10%. This type of 'good business' was accepted without any further questions or explanations needed (Shaplen 1960; Glete 1981).

Kreuger became known as a trustworthy person and reliable profit-maker regardless of the business cycles. When war-ravaged European nations needed large and relatively quick loans, Kreuger was already in a position of being a resourceful financier with significant contacts in the market. Encouraged by the monopoly-building culture, he saw a chance to take control over the match industry. His willingness to take risks helped these circumstances flourish. By using his capacity for problem-solving he could hide eventual unprofitable deals through transferring money between accounts from different companies in the Krueger-group and cover it up. He could avoid detection partly because he was charismatic and the public trusted him, and partly because of the highly undemocratic structure of the business culture. One could say that the goal of profit maximization was, for Kreuger, not only a goal for the corporation but also a goal for his own ego (Braithwaite 1988).

Other dynamic variables at organizational levels were the recruitment of board members and CEOs to the subsidiary companies that was more or less unswervingly loyal to Kreuger or just incompetent in managing a company. For a conspiracy-driven author this variable could give the impression that Kreuger planned to swindle companies long before he was alleged to have done it, by recruiting members that he knew would keep quiet or be too ignorant to understand his plans. To some degree this is true, as in the case of Garanta, who was managed by a person who looked like 'Santa Claus' (Partnoy 2011). But, in general, I do not find this explanation probable for the whole Kreuger-group. We have to be aware that even if Kreuger had some exceptional cognitive capacities, he also had negatively corresponding capacities through his lack of empathy inability to show emotion, and his poor organizational skills. He probably could not recruit the right man for the right job, and by his attitude of discrete politeness and even shyness (probably related to his fear of conflict) he recruited those who seemed to be the most eager to work for the financial 'wizard'. Other people, who demonstrated both competence and those who had the experience to run a company such as Lee, Higginson & Co. board members or board members in the Swedish banking system, were loyal to Kreuger because of his calm manner, his charisma and his reliability to deliver profits.

THE CONSEQUENCES

There are just a few examples of the consequences of his risky business and swindles which are best illustrated when Kreuger took over the Estonian match market in 1928. The overtake was managed through a typical two-front strategy of Kreuger, first through a price competition when STAB prohibited Estonian match producers to get into the British market to secure STAB's own market shares. Secondly, by over taking each of the Estonian match factories by a straw man under direct direction of Kreuger. In all this lead to an increase of match prices by three times, and an increase of two times of the Estonian living expenses. Simultaneously, as the number of labor forces in all the Estonian match factories decreased by nine times (from 450 to 50 workers), the Estonian match production was obliterated and the match production was replaced by imports from Sweden (Wikander 1977). With no specific numbers for other nations it's hard to say what the consequences were exactly. However, taking the Estonian match market as an example of Kreuger's match monopoly strategy, the effect must have been considerable because the price increase of matches pressing living expenses and the rationalization of decreasing labor force were two standing elements in Kreuger's strategy.

However, the deepest social consequences of Kreuger's business strategy were most likely given in the financial field, especially through the damages caused by Kreuger & Toll going bankrupt in 1932. The Swedish banking system, which had

lent large sums of money, were not damaged; they got their accumulated values and money back. Also, several big business
leaders in Swedish business such as Axel Wenner-Gren and
Marcus Wallenberg even made a substantial profit in the bankruptcy of the Kreuger-group. However, private investors (mostly from the middle class) were reimbursed only 0.0798% of the
total debt of 1 billion skr by the bankrupt estate (Arlebäck
2000; Shaplen 1960). According to Arlebäck, the majority of
the private investors were from America and England and only
a small part from Sweden. Yet, according to Shaplen, the majority of the private investors were middle class Swedes, roughly indicated by their annual tax declarations showing a 10% decrease of their capital income as a group. In fact, counting on
the decrease of capital income from 1931 to 1933 when the aftermath of Kreuger's fall was most notable, the decrease was
15.34% ,a decrease from 414.7 million skr to 350.8 million skr
(*Historisk statistik för Sverige Statistiska översiktstabeller,*
1960). According to the report on living conditions and house-
hold income (*Levnadsvillkor och hushållsvanor i städer och in-*
dustriorter omkring år 1933, 1938:49) this decrease in capital
income had no significant effect on the living conditions for
households, but for the Swedish companies, they experienced a
drastic income of capital decrease of 67.7% between 1931-1932
(*Historisk statistik för Sverige Statistiska översiktstabeller,*
1960).

However, the known consequences of the Kreuger crash are
the legal consequences. In USA, the Securities Act of 1933 introduced by President Franklin D. Roosevelt was a direct consequence of the Price Waterhouse Coopers report on Kreuger.
This act stated that the investor's primary goal was to ensure
that they gave complete and truthful information on the securities they offered to sell, something that Ivar Kreuger's business
plan did not do. The year after, the Securities Exchange Act of
1934 was introduced to forbid buying and selling orders that
had too rapid a turnover, which gave the impression of active
trading (Clikeman 2009). This was a specialty that Kreuger
used in many of his emissions over the years. Also, in Sweden,
the Kreuger crash led to legal consequences such as the introduction of The Companies Act of 1944, which stated that public accountants should become compulsory in listed companies,

signing the balance sheet in the single company as well as between the parent company and its subsidiaries (Wallerstedt 2001).

REFERENCES

Alvesalo, A., and S. Tombs. 2002. "Working for Criminalization of Economic Offending: Contradictions for Critical Criminology?" *Critical Criminology* 11(1): 21–40. doi:10.1023/A:1021126217510

Alvesalo, A., S. Tombs, E. Virta, and D. Whyte. 2006. "Re-Imagining Crime Prevention: Controlling Corporate Crime?" *Crime, Law and Social Change* 45(1): 1–25. doi:10.1007/s10611-005-9004-2

Arlebäck, S. O. 2000. *Kreugerkraschen: storbankernas verk?* Skanör: Wallgård.

Babiak, P., C. S. Neumann, and R. D. Hare. 2010. "Corporate Psychopathy: Talking the Walk." *Behavioral Sciences & the Law* 28(2): 174–193. doi:10.1002/bsl.925

Bjerre, P. 1932. *Kreuger.* Stockholm: Natur och kultur.

Braithwaite, J. 1988. "White-Collar Crime, Competition, and Capitalism: Comment on Coleman." *American Journal of Sociology* 94(3): 627–632. doi:10.2307/2780256

Byttner, Anders. (1951). *Arvet efter Ivar Kreuger.* Natur och Kultur.

Cederschiöld, G. 1937. *Tretton år med Ivar Kreuger.* Stockholm: Natur och kultur.

Clikeman, P. M. 2009. *Called to Account: Fourteen Financial Frauds that Shaped the American Accounting Profession.* New York: Routledge. Hämtad från http://catdir.loc.gov/catdir/toc/ecip0822/2008028151.html

DeKeseredy, W. S. and B. Perry. 2006. *Advancing Critical Criminology: Theory And Application.* Lanham: Lexington Books.

Eddy, G. A. 1937. "Security Issues and Real Investment in 1929." *The Review of Economics and Statistics* 19(2): 79–91. doi:10.2307/1928241

Farrington, D. P. 2008. *Integrated Developmental and Life-Course Theories of Offending* (Advances in Criminological Theory). Brunswick: Transaction Publishers.

Flesher, D. L. and T. K. Flesher. 1986. "Ivar Kreuger's Contribution to U.S. Financial Reporting." *The Accounting Review* 61(3): 421–434. doi:10.2307/247150

Friedrichs, D. 2004. "Enron Et Al.: Paradigmatic White Collar Crime Cases for the New Century." *Critical Criminology* 12(2): 113–132. doi:10.1023/B:CRIT.0000040258.21821.39

Galbraith, J. K. 2009. *The Great Crash of 1929*. New York: Houghton Mifflin Harcourt.

Glete, J. 1981. *Kreugerkoncernen och krisen på svensk aktiemarknad: The Kreuger group and the crisis on the Swedish stock market: studier om svenskt och internationellt riskkapital under mellankrigstiden*. Stockholm: Almqvist & Wiksell International.

Gäfvert, B. 1979. *Kreuger, riksbanken och regeringen: [Kreuger, Sveriges Riksbank and the Swedish Government]*. Stockholm: LiberFörlag.

Hassbring, L. 1979. *The International Development of the Swedish Match Company, 1917-1924*. Stockholm: LiberFörlag.

Historisk statistik för Sverige Statistiska översiktstabeller: utöver i del I och del II publicerade t.o.m. år 1950. Statistical survey. 1960. Örebro: Statistiska centralbyrån (SCB).

Ingham, G. 2013. *Capitalism: With a New Postscript on the Financial Crisis and Its Aftermath*. New York: John Wiley & Sons.

Kumar, G., D. Flesher, and T. Flesher. 2007. *Ivar Kreuger Reborn: A Swedish/American Accounting Fraud Resurfaces in Italy and India* (SSRN Scholarly Paper No. ID 1025525). Rochester, NY: Social Science Research Network. Hämtad från http://papers.ssrn.com/abstract=1025525

Lasslett, K. 2010. "Scientific Method and the Crimes of the Powerful." *Critical Criminology* 18(3): 211–228. doi:10.1007/s10612-010-9100-1

Laub, J. H. and R. J. Sampson. 2003. *Shared Beginnings, Divergent lives: Delinquent Boys to Age 70*. Cambridge, MA: Harvard University Press.

Levnadsvillkor och hushållsvanor i städer och industriorter omkring år 1933: [Les budgets de ménage dans les villes et dans les agglomérations industrielles vers 1933]. 1938. Stockholm.

Lindgren, Hå. (1982). The Kreuger Crash of 1932 in memory of a financial genius, or was he a simple swindler? *Scandinavian Economic History Review, 30*(3), 189–206. doi:10.1080/03585522.1982.10407986

Lönnborg, M., A. Ögren, and M. Rafferty. 2011. "Banks and Swedish Financial Crises in the 1920s and 1930s." *Business History* 53(2): 230–248. doi:10.1080/00076791.2011.555108

Mills, C. W. 1971. *Makteliten*. Stockholm: Rabén & Sjögren.

Partnoy, F. 2011. *Tändstickskungen Ivar Kreuger: århundradets finansskandal*. Stockholm: Månpocket.

———. 2010. *Historical Perspectives on the Financial Crisis: Ivar Kreuger, the Credit-Rating Agencies, and Two Theories About the Function, and Dysfunction, of Markets* (SSRN Scholarly Paper No. ID 1547201).

Rochester, NY: Social Science Research Network. Hämtad från http://papers.ssrn.com/abstract=1547201

Piquero, A. R., D. P. Farrington, and A. Blumstein. 2007. *Key Issues in Criminal Career Research: New Analyses of the Cambridge Study in Delinquent Development*. New York: Cambridge University Press. Hämtad från http://www.loc.gov/catdir/enhancements/fy0642/2006011725-d.html

Scott, M. B. and S. M. Lyman. 1968. "Accounts." *American Sociological Review* 33(1): 46–62. doi:10.2307/2092239

Shaplen, R. and J. K. Galbraith. 1960. *Kreuger, Genius and Swindler*. New York: Knopf.

Slapper, G. and S. Tombs. 1999. *Corporate Crime*. London: Longman Group United Kingdom.

Thunholm, L.-E. 2003. *Ivar Kreuger*. Rimbo: Fischer & Co.

Tombs, S. and D. Whyte. 2003. "Unmasking the Crimes of the Powerful." *Critical Criminology* 11(3): 217–236. doi:10.1023/B:CRIT.0000005811.87302.17

Trolle, U. af. 1992. *Bröderna Kreuger: Torsten och Ivar*. Stockholm: Svenska dagbladet.

Wikander, U. 1977. *Ivar Kreugers tändsticksmonopol 1925-1930: fem fallstudier av marknadskontroll genom statsmonopol*.

Williams, J. 2008. "The lessons of 'Enron': Media Accounts, Corporate Crimes, and Financial Markets." *Theoretical Criminology* 12(4): 471–499. doi:10.1177/1362480608097153

Wozniak, J. 2009. "C. Wright Mills and Higher Immorality: Implications for Corporate Crime, Ethics, and Peacemaking Criminology." *Crime, Law and Social Change* 51(1): 189–203. doi:10.1007/s10611-008-9151-3

[arts & culture]

Art in the Movements Against Extraction Industries

COVER ARTIST: FANNY AISHAA

"The Healing Walk, 2013" Original artwork by Fanny Aishaa. 36"X48". Acrylics. (January 2014.) Based on a photo by Mario Jean/"MADOC", from the video, "Bloquons les sables bitumineux / Let's block the tar sands":
https://vimeo.com/70880413

On our cover this issue, this original piece (first published by *Radical Criminology*) is a painting inspired by the annual Healing Walk at Fort McMurray to raise awareness with the movement against the tar sands.

http://www.healingwalk.org/

From their website:

> The tar sands are growing out of control, destroying the
> climate for all Canadians and poisoning the water of
> everyone living downstream.
>
> ...
>
> On July 5 & 6 2013 a different kind of event took place
> in Northern Alberta in the heart of the destruction. The
> 4th Annual Healing Walk was an opportunity for peo-
> ple from all walks of life to join First Nations and
> Metis in a spiritual gathering that will focus on healing
> the land and the people who are suffering from tar
> sands expansion.
>
> *The Healing Walk is sponsored by the Keepers of*
> *the Athabasca. Keepers of the Athabasca is a collection*
> *of First Nations, Metis, Inuit, environmental groups,*
> *and watershed citizens working together for the protec-*
> *tion of water, land and air, and thus for all living*
> *things today and tomorrow in the Athabasca River Wa-*
> *tershed.*

'No Pipelines on Unceded Wet'suwet'en Territory'

EXCERPTS FROM: HTTP://UNISTOTENCAMP.COM

66 The Unist'ot'en Camp is a resistance community whose purpose is to protect sovereign Wet'suwet'en territory from several proposed pipelines from the Tar Sands Gigaproject and shale gas from Hydraulic Fracturing Projects in the Peace River Region.

Wet'suwet'en territory, which extends from Burns Lake to the Coastal Mountains, is sovereign territory which has never been ceded to the colonial Canadian state; the Wet'suwet'en are not under treaty with the Canadian government. Their territory, therefore, is and always will be free, and belongs to the Wet'-suwet'en people alone.

Since July of 2010, the Wet'suwet'en have established a camp in the pathway of the Pacific Trails Pipeline. Likhts'amisyu hereditary chief Toghestiy states

> Unist'ot'en and Grassroots Wet'suwet'en have consistently stated that they will not allow such a pipeline to pass through their territo-ry. The federal and provincial governments, as well as Indian Act tribal councils or bands, have no right or jurisdiction to approve de-velopment on Unist'ot'en lands. By consulting only with elected In-dian Act tribal councils and bands, the Canadian government breaks its own laws as outlined in the 1997 Supreme Court of Canada Del-gamuukw decision which recognizes Hereditary adjudication pro-cesses.

[◄opposite page, "No Pipelines" photo/reproduction of artwork, painted on his drum by Toghestiy, text added by VicFan.]

[▶ "Mintselh", nighthawk/watcher,
    a crest of the Unist'ot'ten, drawn by
    Likhts'amisyu hereditary chief
    Toghestiy (2013). He says of this
    'supernatural' bird, "it flies nonstop through
    their lands and keeps an eye out for
    trespassers. It never lands thus it
    has no legs."]

Freda Huson, spokeswoman for the Unist'ot'en Clan, states:

> Pacific Trails Pipeline does not have permission to be on our terri-
> tory. This is unceded land. Through emails and in meetings, we
> have repeatedly said NO. Pacific Trail Pipeline's proposed route is
> through two main salmon spawning channels which provide our
> staple food supply. We have made the message clear to Pacific
> Trails, Enbridge, and all of industry: We will not permit any pipe-
> lines through our territory.

The Unist'ot'en clan is against all pipelines slated to cross
through their territories. This includes Enbridge Northern
Gateway, Pacific Trails, Coast Gas Link, Kinder Morgan's
northern proposal, and others. Pacific Trails Pipeline is the
most pressing and immediate threat to the community. The
Enbridge pipeline [as proposed] would be built side by side—
with essentially the same right of way as Pacific Trails—thus
raising concerns that the Pacific Trails Pipeline might 'blaze a
trail' for the Enbridge project.

HOW TO SUPPORT: The Unis'tot'en camp stands directly in
the path of the proposed pipelines. As long as it stands, no
pipelines can be built. By supporting the camp, you are not only
helping grassroots Wet'suwet'en assert their sovereign right to
live on their unceded traditional territories, you are also helping
to put a stop to the eco-cidal expansion of tar sands and shale
gas projects through the creation of a so-called "energy
corridor."

DONATE: Operating the camp daily requires fuel, materials, food, and resources of all sorts, and for that we need your help. Resistance is a collective effort and calls for the support of the entire community. Please donate to camp, all contributions are greatly appreciated.

VicFAN Unist'ot'en Solidarity Page: wildcoast.ca/caravan

We can also accept email transfers at <**fhuson@gmail.com**>
Or cheques can be sent to *Tse Wedi Elth (Rocks Flowing),
620 CN Station Rd, Smithers, BC, V0J 2N1.*

99

[▲ "No Enbridge." Drawing by Gord Hill (2011)]

Support the Mi'kmaq Land Defenders' Stand at Elsipogtog

[See in full colour on our website.]

Portrait of Amanda Polchies, holding an eagle feather. Painting by Fanny Aishaa, based on a photo taken October 17, 2013 at Elsipogtog (New Brunswick) by Ossie Michelin/APTN/twitter: @osmich.

This was during a standoff between advancing Royal Canadian Mounted Police against Mi'kmaq land defenders, who have been engaged in a heated struggle to protect their land and water from hydraulic fracturing ("fracking") by Texas-based gas giant SWN Resources." The photo itself has been widely shared, an iconic symbol of resistance to destructive industrial development—and of women's role in fighting for the water.

Artist Fanny Aishaa says of the painting,

> Thanks goes to these guardians of the Earth, voices that need to be listened to... While all the media has been focusing on the [Quebec government's] "Charter of Values" and the importance of female and male equality, it is the first female entity, Mother Earth, the source of all lives, whose needs are forgotten in the pursuit of economic development policies. Care for water, air, the Earth itself, these are the true values for urgent focus. When the territory is in harmony, when health is respected in all its diversity, then humans are also.

[▲ Drawing by Gord Hill (2013)]

This image, from Submedia.tv went viral along with videos from the front lines of the police aggression against their line on the Highway 134 in October (also shot by the 'Stimulator')...

THE CROWN CALLS THEM CRIMINALS

Aaron FRANCIS   Germain BREAULT   Jason AUGUSTINE

Coady STEVENS   James PICTOU   David MAZEROLLE

WE CALL THEM HEROES!
SUPPORT THE MI'KMAQ WARRIORS
IMPRISONED FOR DEFENDING YOUR WATER
bit.ly/mikmaqwarriors

In January 2014, Mi'kmaq Warriors began a speaking tour of the West coast, seeking to build support for their movement. You can learn more via several different sites:

Sacred Fire: The People United Against Fracking, #Elsipogtog and Kent County, New Brunswick – http://sacredfirenb.com/ SacredFireNB@gmail.com

or see   warriorpublications.wordpress.com/tag/
                    mikmaq-warrior-society/

Send donations to support! Cheques can be mailed to
mikmaw warrior society
Po box 7739 eskasoni ns b1w1b8

More Submedia Videos...

Mi'kmaq Blockade (video): http://www.submedia.tv/stimulator/ 2013/10/16/mikmaq_blockade/

Crisis in Elsipogtog (Photo essay): http://www.submedia.tv/ stimulator/2013/10/17/crisis-in-elsipogtog/

It's a great day to be Indigenous (video of a speech by Suzanne Patles: http://www.submedia.tv/ stimulator/2013/10/19/its-a-great-day-to-be-indigenous/

Showdown at highway 134 (video): http://www.submedia.tv/ stimulator/2013/10/20/showdown-at-highway-134/

Submedia also teamed up with Indigenous organizer Amanda Lickers to produce

Kahsatstenhsera:
Indigenous Resistance to Tar Sands Pipelines

Kahsatstenhsera gah-sad-sdanh-se-ra is a Kanienkeha:ka (Mohawk) word that means Strength in Unity. This short documentary details contemporary Indigenous resistance to tar sands pipeline expansion, in particular the Line 9 and Energy East pipelines, which threaten the health of our territories in the northeast of Turtle Island. It includes the voices and perspectives of Dene, Wolastiqiyik, Mi'kmaq, Anishinaabe, Haudenosaunee and Wet'suwet'en land defenders.

See it and find more background info at:

reclaimturtleisland.com

□ ◊ □□ ◊ □□ ◊ □

no one is illegal

كوئى بھى شخص غير قانونى نہيں ہے

personne n'est illégal

कोबज़ाही व्यक्ती कायद्यान्च्या बाहेर नाही.

NO BORDERS!

STOP DEPORTATIONS

هيچ كسى غير قانونى نيست

geen mens is illegaal

எவரும் சட்ட விரோதமானவர்கள் அல்ல.

NINGUNA PERSONA ES ILEGAL

hiç bir kimse oturumsuz değil

0}3ஞ ।ඥ: ५58: ५38hgo

kein mensch ist illegal

sort of in clockwise order:

urdu
french
marathi
tamil
spanish
punjabi
cantonese
german
amharic
hungarian
dutch
persian
english...

没有人是非法的

ਏਹ ਦੀ ਨਾਜਾਇਜ਼ ਨਹੀਂ ਹੈ

nooneisillegal.org

[insurgencies]

The Color of Corporate Corrections, Part II: Contractual Exemptions and the Overrepresentation of People of Color in Private Prisons

CHRISTOPHER PETRELLA[1]

My previous study[2] published in *Radical Criminology,* (Issue 2, Fall 2013) demonstrates that people of color[3]–though historically overrepresented in public prisons relative to their share of state and national populations–are *further* overrepresented in private prisons contracted by departments of correction in Arizona, California, and Texas.

My current research on the relationship between U.S. racial formation and prison privatization enlarges my previous work by foregrounding the question of *why.* That is, *why is it that people of color are overrepresented in private versus public fa-*

---

[1] Christopher Petrella is a doctoral candidate in African American Studies at U.C. Berkeley. His dissertation is entitled *"Race, Markets, and the Rise of the Private Prison State."* Learn more at www.christopherfrancispetrella.net

[2] "The Color of Corporate Corrections." Radical Criminology (2) http://journal.radicalcriminology.org/index.php/rc/article/view/27

[3] Although racial designations are always imprecise, elusive, historically situated, and subject to revision, I have appropriated U.S. Census Bureau racial categories for the purposes of this study to preserve nomenclatural, and therefore statistical, fidelity in cross referencing figures. People of color here are defined as "Black, American Indian or Alaska Native, Asian, Native Hawaiian or Pacific Islander, and non-white Hispanic or Latino."

*cilities in select states even in the absence of explicit racially
discriminatory correctional placement or classification policies?*

In order to explain why people of color tend to be overrepresented in private relative to public facilities around the country
this study draws on data from nine (9) states: Arizona, California, Colorado, Georgia, Mississippi, Ohio, Oklahoma, Tennessee, and Texas. These states were selected on the basis of their
reliably large sample size. Each of the nine states considered
currently houses at least 3,000 prisoners in private minimum
and/or medium security facilities.[4] Additionally, this study con-
trols for differences in facility population profile. Therefore,
only public and private facilities/units with a minimum and/or
medium security designation are included in this comparison.
And finally, as in my previous work, in order to avoid artificial-
ly inflating the over-incarceration of people of color in for-prof-
it prisons this examination intentionally excludes figures from
federal detention centers controlled by U.S. Immigration and
Customs Enforcement (ICE), the U.S. Marshals Service, and
detention facilities managed at the local level. For similar reasons, it strategically excludes data from transfer centers, work
release centers, community corrections facilities, and reception
centers.

Based on an analysis of data obtained from over sixty sepa-
rate public record requests[5] and reports accessible on state department of corrections websites, this study finds that people of
color are overrepresented in private minimum and/or medium
security private facilities relative to their public counterparts in
each of the nine (9) states examined.

This research further posits that the overrepresentation of
people of color in private versus public prisons across the country is primarily attributable to an unlikely source: finely tailored
contractual provisions that implicitly exempt private prison

---

[4] Over thirty states in total contract with private prison companies but many of
these jurisdictions have sample sizes that are statistically insignificant.
Alaska, for instance, houses less than 1,000 prisoners in minimum and/or
medium security private facilities.

[5] All public record requests were made between May, 2012 and September,
2013.

companies from housing certain types of individuals whose health care and staffing costs disproportionately attenuate profit margins. *Health—and therefore age—tends to serve as a proxy for race without any explicit reference to it.*

These figures suggest that the older the prisoner, the more likely that prisoner is to be "Non-Hispanic, white." Correspondingly, the younger the prisoner, the more likely that prisoner is to be a person of color. Most prisoners over 50 today were convicted and sentenced before the operationalization of the so-called "War on Drugs," a skein of policies that have disproportionately criminalized communities of color. By implication, the vast majority of those incarcerated prior to 1980—both in real numbers and on a percentage basis— was "Non-Hispanic, white."[6] Contrastingly, black individuals constituted 30 percent of state prisons admits in 1950, 34 percent in 1960, roughly 40 percent in 1970, and 42 percent by 1980.[7]

Therefore, age and health serve as dual proxies for race when explaining the persistent racial disparities in private versus public facilities with similar population profiles.

Elderly and/or geriatric prisoners tend to cost more to incarcerate. A 2012 ACLU report estimates that it costs $34,135 per year to house a non-geriatric prisoner, but it costs $68,270 per year to house a prisoner age 50 and older.[8]

My study firmly suggests that private prison management companies[9] responsible for providing health services exempt themselves contractually from accepting and housing prisoners with chronic medical conditions as well as those whose health care costs will be "above average."[10] This fact results in a pris-

---

[6] For example, an individual convicted in 1970 as a 20 year-old would be 63 today. Research conducted by the U.S. Department of Justice and the ACLU both conclude that prisoners over the age of 50 are most likely to be "non-Hispanic, white." https://www.ncjrs.gov/pdffiles1/nij/125618.pdf

[7] Ibid.

[8] https://www.aclu.org/files/assets/elderlyprisonreport_20120613_1.pdf

[9] Corrections Corporation of America, the GEO Group, and MTC are the three largest private prison companies in the United States. Together they constitute close to 90 percent of the private corrections market share.

[10] Please consider these examples of contractual exemptions. **Note California:** "In the event that the CDCR requests that the contractor [Corrections Corporation of America] accept offenders with serious or

oner profile that is far younger and far "darker" in minimum and/or medium security private facilities than in select counterpart public facilities. In fact, the states in which the private versus public racial disparities are most pronounced also happen to be the states in which the private versus public age disparities are most salient. Please see data on Oklahoma and Texas.

Secondly, on the rare occasion that a state department of correction retains control of health services while contracting

---

significant mental health or serious or significant physical problems, included but not limited to physical disability, CDCR and the contractor shall mutually agree to an appropriate plan of care and the population and the allocation of costs associated therewith. If the overall percentage of offenders requiring Hepatitis C treatment exceeds the overall percentage of offenders requiring Hepatitis C treatment in the CDCR system, CDCR agrees to pay the treatment costs for those offenders in excess of the percentage of offenders requiring Hepatitis C treatment in the CDCR system…The cost of providing on-site medical, mental health or dental services through facility staff or contracted services shall be considered normal costs incidental to the operation of the facility and is included in the CDCR offender per diem rates, except that the CDCR shall pay for…all expenses in excess of $2,500 annually per inmate for medically necessary, off site hospital or emergency care…all HIV or AIDS related inpatient and outpatient medical costs and the costs of providing AZT or other medications therapeutically indicated and medically necessary for the treatment of offenders with HIV or AIDS." **Note Oklahoma:** "The contractor [The GEO Group] will be responsible for the treatment of offenders infected with HIV. This will include, but will not be limited to, all in-patient and outpatient medical costs excluding the cost of providing antiviral medications therapeutically indicated for the treatment of HIV. If the number of the HIV positive offender population being treated increases by 10 offenders then the medication cost allocation shall be subject to negotiation. The contractor may return any offender diagnosed with AIDS, as defined the center for disease control to the state. The contractor is responsible for treatment of Hepatitis C offenders in accordance with the Oklahoma DOC protocol. If the number of Hepatitis C positive offender population being treated at any one time is more than two (2) then the DOC will transfer those additional offenders out of the facility. When an offender reaches end stage Hepatitis C and can no longer be treated at the contractor's facility, the DOC will transfer the offender out of the facility…The contractor may claim reimbursement from the department for the inpatient hospitalization in a licensed hospital, for the hospital charges only, not separate physician or other provider charges, for the amount which exceeds 50,000 per inpatient hospital discharge for each single hospital stay which originates while the contract for services is in effect between the contractor and the department." **Note Mississippi:** "MTC [Management and Training Company] will not be responsible or liable for providing counseling and/or mental health programs. MTC will not be responsible or liable for providing medical, mental health, optometry, pharmaceutical, dental, or similar services. MDOC shall provide with a private prison management company[11] elderly populations still remain disproportionately expensive to incarcerate because those assigned to monitor geriatric and/or chronically ill prisoners often require special training, benefit from higher pay grades, and are assigned at lower staff-to-prisoner ratios. Each of these considerations further erodes profit margins.

In sum, explicit contractual exemptions for health services and implicit provisions for reducing "high cost" geriatric or infirmed prisoners helps to explain ongoing racial disparities in private versus public prisons with similar population profiles. My modest hope is that this study provides an incontrovertible example of the ways in which seemingly "race neutral" or "colorblind" carceral policies continue to have a differential impact on communities of color.[12]

---

security and control of inmates for outpatient needs and /or hospitalization."
Note Arizona: According to a 2011 report issued by the Arizona Department of Corrections "Both private and state-run prison units have differences in the types of inmates that can be housed based on inmate medical, mental health and dental needs Generally, state-run prisons house a higher percentage of inmates with higher medical and mental health needs than private prison units. Private prison units considered to be corridor facilities have access to off-site healthcare and can house inmates with more severe medical and mental health needs. Additionally, two private contracts have a $10,000 cap per inmate on health care services. When the health care cost of a single inmate exceeds this cap, the inmate is returned to a state-run prison unit and the state assumes all further medical treatment costs associated with the inmate. The consolidation of inmates with higher medical and mental health needs to certain units is cost-efficient overall, but results in a higher per diem cost for those units and complexes that house these inmates."
http://www.azcorrections.gov/ARS41_
1609_01_Biennial_Comparison_Report122111_e_v.pdf

[11] In Texas, for instance, medical care in private prisons is provided by Correctional Managed Health Care, a public agency.

[12] The overrepresentation of people of color in private prisons indicates they are disproportionately siphoned away from public prisons—precisely the types of facilities that provide the greatest access to educational and rehabilitative programs and services. http://www.urban.org/projects/reentry-roundtable/upload/Crayton.pdf. People of color continue to be seen in the national imagination as sources of profit extraction and not necessarily as citizens deserving of public services.

Data:

Arizona: Public Minimum/Medium Security Facilities or Units (People of Color / Total Population)

Douglas-Gila: 359/601

Douglas-Mohave: 663/930

Douglas-Eggers: 127/231

Florence-East: 397/690

Florence-North: 604/1085

Florence-Globe: 164/293

Lewis-Stiner: 786/1176

Lewis-Sunrise: 42/99

Safford-Fort Grant: 331/573

Safford-Graham: 349/536

Safford-Tonto: 194/306

Tucson-Cimarron: 246/371

Tucson-Santa Rita: 503/777

Tucson-Winchester: 501/769

Tucson-Catalina: 144/348

Tucson-Whetstone: 685:1171

Winslow-Coronado: 318/498

Winslow-Kaibab: 614/775

Winslow-Apache: 212/358

Yuma-Cheyenne: 734/1188

Yuma-Cocopah: 570/1047

Yuma-Cibola: 152/308

Yuma-La Paz: 661/864

62 % ■
Percent population People of Color

Arizona Public Facilities

13 % ■
Percent population age 50 or older

Arizona Public Facilities

ARIZONA: PRIVATE MINIMUM/MEDIUM SECURITY FACILITIES OR UNITS (PEOPLE OF COLOR / TOTAL POPULATION)

Kingman-Cerbat: 1193/1965
Kingman-Hualapal: 1069/1512
Marana: 309/496

65 % ■
Percent population People of Color

Arizona Private Facilities

11 % ■
Percent population age 50 or older

Arizona Private Facilities

CALIFORNIA: PUBLIC MINIMUM/MEDIUM SECURITY FACILITIES OR UNITS (PEOPLE OF COLOR / TOTAL POPULATION)

Avenal: 4447/6217

California Men's Colony: 4719/6240

California Men's Rehabilitation Center: 3156/4263

Chuckawalla / Ironwood: 6221/7634

Folsom: 5360/6676

76 % ■
Percent population People of Color

California Public Facilities

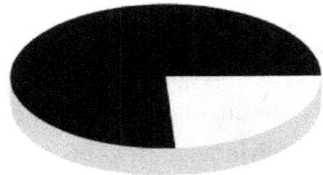

*Note: Though the California Department of Corrections and Rehabilitation has been incredibly uncooperative in releasing data pertaining to the proportion of prisoners age 50 and older in minimum/medium-security public and private facilities, readers should note that the publicly-operated California Health Care facility in Stockton, CA is the only facility officially charged with the task of "housing for patients who require acute and long-term care for medical or psychiatric needs." It is therefore reasonable to hypothesize that this particular publicly-operated facility would contain the highest proportion of prisoners age 50 and older among California's more than 30 state-operated prisons.

http://cdcrtoday.blogspot.com/2013/06/cdcr-dedicates-new-california- health.html

CALIFORNIA: PRIVATE (OUTSOURCED) MINIMUM/MEDIUM SECURITY FACILITIES OR UNITS (PEOPLE OF COLOR / TOTAL POPULATION)

> La Palma (in Arizona): 2454/2949
> North Fork (in Oklahoma): 1774/2003
> Red Rock (in Arizona): 1382/1504
> Tallahatchie (in Mississippi): 2410/2603

89 % ■
Percent population People of Color

California Private Facilities

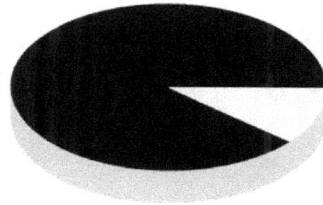

COLORADO: PUBLIC MINIMUM/MEDIUM SECURITY FACILITIES OR UNITS (PEOPLE OF COLOR / TOTAL POPULATION)

> Arkansas Valley: 575/1008
> Buena Vista: 546/926
> Fremont: 798/1662

53 % ■
Percent population People of Color

Colorado Public Facilities

23 % ■
Percent population Age 50 or Older

Colorado Public Facilities

COLORADO: PRIVATE MINIMUM/MEDIUM SECURITY FACILITIES OR UNITS (PEOPLE OF COLOR / TOTAL POPULATION)

Bent: 764/1317

Crowley: 938/1590

Kit Carson: 456/800

58 % ■
Percent population People of Color

Colorado Private Facilities

16 % ■
Percent population Age 50 or Older

Colorado Private Facilities

GEORGIA: PUBLIC MINIMUM/MEDIUM SECURITY FACILITIES OR UNITS (PEOPLE OF COLOR / TOTAL POPULATION)

Autry: 1155/1644
Calhoun: 1169/1635
Central: 614/1099
Dodge: 796/1198
Dooly: 1093/1652
Johnson State: 855/1544
Lee State: 523/725
Long: 100/224
Montgomery: 236/374

65 % ■
Percentage People of Color

Georgia Public Facilities

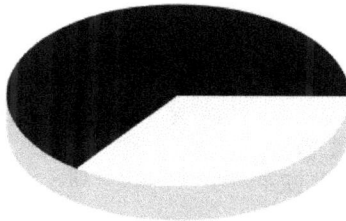

21 % ■
Percent population Age 50 or Older

Georgia Public Facilities

GEORGIA: PRIVATE MINIMUM/MEDIUM SECURITY FACILITIES OR UNITS (PEOPLE OF COLOR / TOTAL POPULATION)

Coffee: 1811/2540
Jenkins: 665/1107
Riverbend: 1012/1459
Wheeler: 1817/2640

68 % ■
Percentage People of Color

Georgia Private Facilities

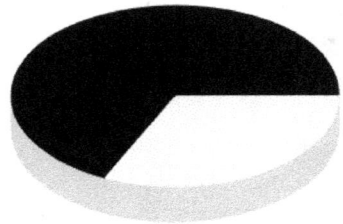

15 % ■
Percent population Age 50 or Older

Georgia Private Facilities

MISSISSIPPI: PUBLIC MINIMUM/MEDIUM SECURITY FACILITIES OR UNITS (PEOPLE OF COLOR / TOTAL POPULATION)*

CMCF: 1451/2188

66 % ■
Percentage People of Color

Mississippi Public Facility

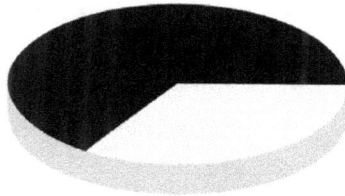

MISSISSIPPI: PRIVATE MEDIUM SECURITY FACILITIES (PEOPLE OF COLOR / TOTAL POPULATION)*

as Composite Totals: 3256/4314

75 % ■
Percentage People of Color

Mississippi Private Facilities

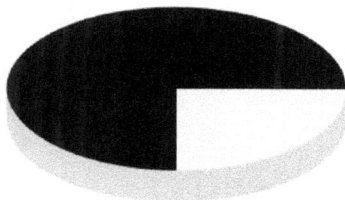

*Note: Though the Mississippi Department of Corrections has not been able to provide me with data pertaining to the proportion of prisoners age 50 and older in minimum/medium-security public and private facilities, readers should note that the *publicly-operated* Mississippi State Penitentiary in Parchman, MS is the only facility responsible for "maintain[ing] two special units for its elderly prisoners."— http://www.mdoc.state.ms.us

OHIO: PUBLIC MINIMUM/MEDIUM SECURITY FACILITIES OR UNITS (PEOPLE OF COLOR / TOTAL POPULATION)

Allen Oakwood: 659/1590

Marion: 1343/2617

Dayton: 315/882

Chillicothe: 1038/2747

London: 1119/2263

Belmont: 1220/2762

Noble: 1034/2495

Southeastern: 853/2055

Pickaway: 919/2165

43 % ■
Percentage People of Color

Ohio Public Facilities

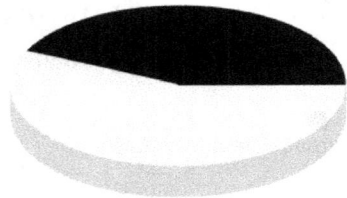

20 % ■
Percent population Age 50 or Older

Ohio Public Facilities

OHIO: PRIVATE MINIMUM/MEDIUM SECURITY FACILITIES OR UNITS (PEOPLE OF COLOR / TOTAL POPULATION)

Lake Erie: 898/1542

North Central Complex: 1113/2708

47 % ■   Ohio Private Facilities
Percentage People of Color

12 % ■   Ohio Private Facilities
Percent population Age 50 or Older

OKLAHOMA: PUBLIC MINIMUM/MEDIUM SECURITY FACILITIES OR UNITS (PEOPLE OF COLOR / TOTAL POPULATION)

Dick Conner: 608/1202

James Crabtree: 387/992

Joseph Harp: 555/1396

Mack Alford: 349/793

OK State Reformatory: 483/1067

44 % ■
Percentage People of Color

Oklahoma Public Facilities

36 % ■
Percent population Age 50 or Older

Oklahoma Public Facilities

OKLAHOMA: PRIVATE MINIMUM/MEDIUM SECURITY FACILITIES OR UNITS (PEOPLE OF COLOR / TOTAL POPULATION)

Davis: 989/1682

Lawton: 1423/2529

57 % ■
Percentage People of Color

Oklahoma Private Facilities

11 % ■
Percent population Age 50 or Older

Oklahoma Private Facilities

TENNESSEE: PUBLIC MINIMUM/MEDIUM SECURITY FACILITIES OR UNITS (PEOPLE OF COLOR / TOTAL POPULATION)

CBCX: 315/604

NWCX: 1315/2404

54 % ■
Percentage People of Color

Tennessee Public Facilities

TENNESSEE: PRIVATE MINIMUM/MEDIUM SECURITY FACILITIES OR UNITS (PEOPLE OF COLOR / TOTAL POPULATION)

Hardeman: 1265/1998

South Central: 765: 1669

Whiteville: 974/1528

58 % ■
Percentage People of Color

Tennessee Private Facilities

* **Note:** Though the Tennessee Department of Correction has stated it "does not have the resources to perform individual requests to disaggregate data [pertaining to the proportion of prisoners age 50 and older in minimum/medium-security public and private facilities]," readers should note that the publicly-operated Lois M. DeBerry Special Needs Facility in Nashville, TN is the only facility responsible for providing "acute and convalescent health care" to Tennessee prisoners. It is therefore reasonable to hypothesize that this particular publicly-operated facility would contain the largest proportion of prisoners age 50 and older among all of Tennessee's prisons.

—http://www.tn.gov/correction/institutions/dsnf.html

TEXAS: PUBLIC MINIMUM/MEDIUM SECURITY FACILITIES OR UNITS (PEOPLE OF COLOR / TOTAL POPULATION)

Byrd: 723/1088
Goree: 483/975
Huntsville: 874/1520
Jester III: 629/1083
Luther: 795/1261
Pack: 763/1429
Powledge: 504/1105
Terrell: 940/1539
Vance: 192/295

57 % ■
Percentage People of Color

Texas Public Facilities

37 % ■
Percent population Age 50 or Older

Texas Public Facilities

TEXAS: PRIVATE MINIMUM/MEDIUM SECURITY FACILITIES OR UNITS (PEOPLE OF COLOR / TOTAL POPULATION)

Billy Moore: 344/499
Bridgeport: 360/520
Cleveland: 361/519
Diboll: 354/517
Estes: 722/1039

69 % ■
Percentage People of Color

Texas Private Facilities

17 % ■
Percent population Age 50 or Older

Texas Private Facilities

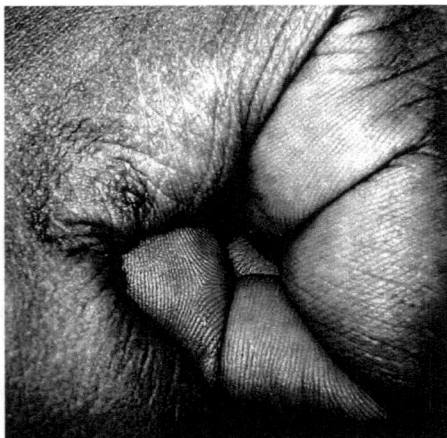

'Fibonacci sequence, the Golden
Mean', photo by Fady Habib
(flickr, CC-BY-2.0)

Jaywalking to Jail: Capitalism, mass incarceration and social control on the streets of Vancouver

AIYANAS ORMOND

In the Downtown Eastside of Vancouver, the Vancouver Area Network of Drug Users (VANDU) is waging a dogged, multi-year campaign against the Vancouver Police Department's practice of using bylaw tickets—particularly for jaywalking, 'street vending', public urination and defecation, and smoking—to criminalize the very poor. Recent freedom of information requests show that 95% of all vending tickets, and 75% of all jaywalking tickets for the entire City of Vancouver are handed out in the Downtown Eastside—evidence of direct targeting of the community's residents.[1]

While this article focuses on the Downtown Eastside, the processes of criminalization of poverty and mass incarceration are not particular to the DTES or to Vancouver. In Toronto, police handed out more than fifteen thousand tickets under the 'Safe Streets Act'; despite declines in panhandling and squeegeeing Toronto police ticketing for these offenses increased at an exponential rate—a 20 fold increase in the past 10 years.[2] Last year a homeless man died in Toronto with more than $30,000 in outstanding tickets.[3] Montreal has gone down

---

[1] Overt physical police violence and murder is also a huge issue in the Downtown Eastside and something VANDU has worked on extensively, but this article focuses on the structural violence embodied in police harassment, ticketing and criminalization of poor people in the neighbourhood.

[2] http://www.homelesshub.ca/caniseeyourID/

[3] http://www.thestar.com/news/gta/2012/09/14/homeless_man_died_owing_more_than_30000_in_fines.html

the same road of 'proactive' policing and in Victoria, police are now charging people gathering returnables from recycling bins with theft.

The criminalization of the poor is supported at the municipal level by police budgets that continue to rise rapidly despite a falling 'crime rate'; at the provincial level by an expansion of prison capacity across the country and increasing numbers of people in remand, especially on 'administration of justice' and drug related charges; and at the federal level by 'tough on crime' mandatory minimum legislation. It is one component of a broad strategy of mass incarceration[4] and social control aimed at the poor, Indigenous people, im/migrant and refugee communities of colour, and labour, environmental, anti-war and anti-capitalist organizers who challenge the system.

There is an urgent need to link the local resistance to these policies of criminalization in different Canadian cities and to build a cross-country network of organizations capable of exposing and opposing them, and linking them to the underlying system of capitalist exploitation and oppression.

COMMUNITY IN THE CROSSHAIRS

It is worth describing in detail how the targeted police harassment of the Downtown Eastside impacts poor people living in this community because people who haven't experienced this level of surveillance, harassment and targeting often don't believe it's real and therefore the tag 'police occupation' seems like hyperbole. But for people who are poor, or Indigenous, or just live in the neighbourhood and don't look like they are 'service providers', it's really not that much of a stretch. And for the thousands of poor people who use drugs—many of them Indigenous people—avoiding, negotiating and suffering police interference is a grinding daily reality.

In addition to a disproportionate share of the patrol cars policing as part of VPD District 2, and drug and vice unit enforcement, the DTES is also subjected to its own neighbourhood police, the 'Beat Enforcement Team' (BET). This is a force of 66 police, whose job is to patrol the Downtown East-

---

[4] http://basicsnews.ca/2011/12/the-mass-incarceration-agenda-in-canada-the-view-from-vancouver/

side on foot, all day, everyday. The VPD's 2009 draft business plan bragged that these BETs would conduct 4 'street checks per cop, per block'. The language of street checks was changed in response to outrage from civil libertarians, so the enforcement of bylaw infractions has become the excuse to stop people, search them, and run their name for warrants.

Here's how it works:

You might come on the police radar because you are engaged in some kind of criminalized survival activity like vending or prostitution, because you are 'known to police' or because you fit the profile of the 'type' of person they are used to policing—especially drug users and low level drug sellers.[5] Because bylaw 'offenses' are often poorly defined, even if you are not actively vending or jaywalking, it isn't difficult for police to identify some infraction by the person they want to target: for example (and these are just some cases I know of) 'leaving the curb unsafely', smoking a cigarette outside of closed business or in an alley, spitting into the street, or transporting goods for sale in a shopping cart.

The bylaw ticket can then be used as a justification to ask for identification and run your name for a warrant for an outstanding criminal, immigration or bylaw issue. This could mean that you go straight to jail, for example for an outstanding drug charge, but more likely for a 'procedural' crime such as a breach of a condition of release. These are conditions that are given out by police based on an arrest and do not require a finding of 'guilt' in court. For example, a VANDU member who is addicted to heroin was recently arrested with 1/10 of 1 gram of heroin. As a condition of his release he was given a 'red zone' (no go) that covers a large part of the Downtown Eastside including the INSITE supervised injection site and areas where he would regularly go to score and shoot drugs, as well as a stipulation that he not be in possession of the drugs, even though he is addicted to heroin and going through withdrawal

---

[5] The retail drug trade is mostly done by people who are addicted to the drugs that they are selling and are paid in drugs, not cash ("sell five rock, get one free"). It's the worst kind of work situation imaginable—these workers are underpaid, have very little back up or support and face violence from both police and bosses (higher up dealers who may be connected to organized crime gangs).

could be life threatening. Thus, even though the possession charge will likely be dropped if and when it ever comes to court, now, if he is stopped by police, he will be arrested and likely charged with a breach—a charge that is much more likely to get him jail time than the original drug charge.[6]

If you haven't already accumulated a warrant you are now in danger of getting one as a result of your ticket. If you do not pay your $250 ticket (and that is more than an entire month's disposable income for someone on the starvation welfare rates in B.C.), you could receive a summons to appear in court. If you receive a summons (or don't receive it, but one is sent to you) and do not appear in court, you could get a warrant for failure to appear, and the next time you interact with the police you'll be charged for this procedural crime that the courts 'take very seriously'.

In a case right in front of VANDU last Summer a VANDU member was 'jacked' up by police in a cruiser that rode right up onto the sidewalk. The police proceeded to have him open his backpack and lay out all his stuff on the ground—lots because he was homeless and staying in a shelter at the time. Having come up with nothing for the search or by running his name the police proceeded to write him a $250 ticket for spitting on the street. He planned on challenging the ticket because he had a number of witnesses to the whole interaction, including me, but he died before he had the chance.

It's impossible to quantify the health impact of the ticketing, the harassment and the repeated interaction with the cops on individuals. It starts with the anger, humiliation and frustration of being targeted for vending when you are poor, or peeing in the alley when you are homeless or don't have access to a toilet in your SRO (single room occupancy) hotel, or jaywalking on your own block like everyone in the world does. It continues to the stress and anxiety of accumulating debts you will never be able to pay, and extends to trying to keep track of summons and potentially a string of court dates if you want to challenge the

---

[6] Administration of justice charges now make up 42% of all court cases in B.C. and accounted for upwards of 20% of admissions to remand (jail) nationally in 2008-2009. The steady growth in this category of charges is the reason that the number of people in prison is increasing even though the crime rate and the crime severity index are decreasing.

ticket. Some folks will actually go to jail on a warrant generated by a bylaw ticket. For others, a series of failure to appear or breach charges can be used to justify being held for months in remand if they are picked up on a more serious charge.[7] And jail is very bad for your health, especially if you are poor, especially if you are a woman with children, especially if you are addicted to drugs or at risk of becoming addicted. In addition to potentially destroying relationships, plans, and housing arrangements, in addition to the deleterious effects on general mental and physical health, incarceration vastly increases your likelihood of contracting hepatitis C and HIV.

Poor and marginalized women have an added vulnerability resulting from this criminalization. A woman who has an outstanding warrant, even one generated from a vending or jaywalking ticket, is much less likely to approach police about a violent husband or boyfriend, or after experiencing violence or threats in the course of selling sex—a reality that was recognized even in Wally Opal's Missing Women Commission of Inquiry.

VENDING

Several blocks of East Hastings are lined by a *de-facto* vendors market where very poor people sell small collections of assorted items on small blankets, or directly on the sidewalk. Most of the items are salvaged by 'binners' (people who go through garbage bins looking for returnables and usable/ saleable items). Probably some of what is sold is boosted or stolen in residential b&e's but a fairly small proportion since a really skilled booster or b&e artist would likely have better channels for moving their goods than camping out on Hastings Street, selling to other poor people.

There is a kind of dance-like quality as the police walk down the block with the vendors rapidly packing up and disappearing into the crowds ten feet ahead of them and then reappearing and redeploying their displays ten feet behind. But the

---

[7] I recently spoke to a guy who had just been released after spending 3 months in remand awaiting a trial for a charge on which he was acquitted. A significant majority of incarceration in Canada is of people who have not actually been convicted of the crime for which they are being jailed!

poetry of it ends as you watch a cop towering over a native elder (two of the VANDU members launching a constitutional challenge to the city's bylaw are native grandmothers) chastising her and giving her a $250 ticket for 'displaying merchandise on the sidewalk'. While the police regularly go on about 'stolen goods' as justification for this criminalization and harassment in the media, they are not actually charging people with theft or possession of stolen property.

In response to the harassment for vending, VANDU, in collaboration with the Downtown Eastside Neighbourhood Council established a weekly vendors market at Pigeon Park in the heart of the DTES. This has become a vibrant community event every Sunday that creates a well organized and community controlled space for the vendors and draws in shoppers from around the neighbourhood and across the city. Despite harassment from the police, supposedly acting on the concerns of recently arrived 'neighbours' living in adjacent gentrified condos, the Pidgeon Park Street Market is thriving and surviving. The demand from VANDU is for the city to redirect funding from police handing out jaywalking tickets (and all the wasteful administrative work associated with the practice) to the community controlled street market, which would allow them to pay a small stipend for volunteers, provide tables to vendors and supply adequate amenities for the vendors and their customers (toilets, water station).

JAYWALKING

Just like most other neighbourhoods there is a lot of jaywalking in the Downtown Eastside. Unlike in other neighbourhoods, if you are poor or look like a drug user you are likely to be criminalized for simply crossing the street. Seventy-five percent of all jaywalking tickets for the entire city of Vancouver are given to poor and oppressed residents of the Downtown Eastside.

Pedestrian safety is actually a huge issue in the Downtown Eastside—not surprising for a community that has a very high proportion of people with disabilities, seniors, people who do not own a car and people who are users of illicit drugs. VANDU has been very concerned about cars striking and killing community members, particularly on Hastings street. VANDU therefore, worked with the City to develop a very good pedestrian safety plan for the neighbourhood, elements of which have been implemented, including a 6 block 30km/hour zone on Hastings.[8]

The Vancouver Police Department took a public position against the 30k zone and have refused to enforce it. Instead they persist on handing out jaywalking tickets, claiming that this is a public safety intervention. Of course, they have no evidence (there is none) that bylaw ticketing either discourages jaywalking or increases pedestrian safety. Rather, the paternalistic pretense covers the real reason for the enforcement which is the chance to check IDs and run names for warrants, to target and harass individuals who are considered 'undesirables', and to generate a perpetually criminalized population, since non-payment of a jaywalking ticket can result in a summons to court and warrant for failure to appear.

MINING THE DOWNTOWN EASTSIDE FOR CRIME

Why do the police so single-mindedly and doggedly pursue this punitive policing approach using bylaw tickets and attack and sabotage any alternative approach to dealing with the 'street disorder' that so offends them?

The VPD characterizes their occupation of the Downtown Eastside as 'proactive' policing and point to supposed success in New York and other jurisdictions as its justification. The proactive (or 'broken windows' model of policing) theorizes that by proactively and aggressively pursuing 'minor' crime and street disorder, police undermine the conditions for criminality and more major crimes. Since it's ascendance in the 1990s the theory has largely been debunked, but what isn't bunk is that poor people, indigenous people, people of colour and people who use illicit drugs, are unfairly and disproportionately targeted under these proactive policing schemes.

Despite being discredited in the research literature, the 'proactive' policing approach remains standard practice within the ranks of the VPD. That's because it fits so well with the institutional interest and self interest of the VPD, its leadership

---

[8] http://www.vandu.org/documents/WereAllPedestrians_EXECUTIVE_SUMMARY.pdf

and individual cops. Policing in Vancouver is big money, and the police budget continues to rise, topping $200 million, or 20% of the total City of Vancouver budget in 2012. Over 650 individual VPD police took home over $100,000 in 2011 and VPD Chief Jim Chu topped $300,000.

VANDU has characterized the police approach in the DTES as 'mining our neighbourhood for crime'. 'Crime' has become the resource on which this $200 million enterprise is built. The top brass and managers can go to the city and demand constantly rising budgets by pointing to 'criminality', 'street disorder' and 'the drug trade'. Individual cops advance their careers and prestige by posting high arrest numbers even if its based on arresting desperately poor and addicted people for crimes like breach of an undertaking or failure to appear in court for a vending ticket.

Outside of TV Drama, the real world of policing in Canada was described by (former Toronto Mayor) John Sewell in his open letter to (current Toronto Mayor) Rob Ford, as "Lots of gravy in bloated police budget".[9] Toronto Police on average respond to one call every two shifts, and make only seven or eight arrests **per year**, only one of which would be for a serious violent crime. In that context police justify their existence (and massive budgets) by 'proactive policing' in areas identified as high crime (i.e. lots of poor people), a self-fulfilling label if you are criminalizing survival activities like vending or street-level drug dealing and repeatedly checking the same people you criminalized last week for outstanding warrants, violations of conditions of release, or failure to appear.

So police constitute a built-in lobby for 'tough on crime' policies at the local level. An industry lobby that relies on the myths of 'inner city crime', of drugs and the drug trade as a 'plague' in our cities and of poor people as scary, 'disorderly', violent and irrational. They don't want to look at involvement in the drug trade and other criminalized activities as a rational response to limited economic opportunities; to drug addiction as a response to trauma, social violence and despair; and to poor communities as functioning, complex and dynamic social networks built on a particular economic base (and in some ways

---

[9] http://www.thestar.com/opinion/editorialopinion/2011/01/05/lots_of_gravy_in_bloated_police_budget.html

less dysfunctional and alienated than the 'mainstream' social order from which they are marginalized).

THE MASS INCARCERATION AGENDA

Across the country there is a huge boom in prison renovation and construction—according to the National Post the largest expansion of prison building 'since the 1930s'.[10] The federal government is adding 2,700 new prison 'beds' and the provinces are adding another 7,000 spaces across the country.[11] The federal expenditure for prisons has ballooned to $2.98 billion this year (a more than 80% increase) and is expected to rise to $3.98 billion next year. When you include the provincial expenditure on prisons the current annual cost is $4.4 billion, expected to rise to $9.5 billion by 2015.

In Alberta, the newly constructed Edmonton Remand Centre is a $586 million, 16-hectare facility that has space for up to 2,800 prisoners. The Toronto South Detention Centre, to replace the Don Jail, carries a price tag of over $1 billion and is being built as a "Public-Private-Partnership" (P3) with a private company to build, design and operate the 1650 bed facility for 30 years.

In British Columbia the Provincial Government is in the process of building a 216-cell, $185 million remand centre in Surrey and has budgeted for an even larger facility (more than 500 cells) in the Okanagan. Both facilities are being built on a 'Private-Public-Partnership' (P3) model. The contract to 'design-build-operate' the Surrey facility has already been awarded to Brookfield Properties Management, a subsidiary of Brookfield Asset Management, a gigantic Canadian real estate corporation that manages $150 billion in assets globally. This company will profit off the incarceration of the poor for the 30 year period of the contract.

The cost of incarceration is about $57,000 per year in a provincial jail and more than $88,000 a year in the federal system. So if you get a mandatory minimum of 1 year for selling drugs,

---

[10] http://news.nationalpost.com/2011/09/24/the-largest-expansion-of-prison-building-since-the-1930s/

[11] http://news.nationalpost.com/2011/09/24/by-the-numbers-how-many-new-prison-beds-are-coming-to-your-part-of-canada/

probably one that you are addicted to, the State will spend $57,000 on you, but if you are unemployed and have to rely on welfare you'll get $7320 per year ($610/ month—the regular welfare rate in B.C.). Since you can't survive on $610, and because welfare will claw back any income you declare, dollar for dollar, you will have to resort to some kind of crime. As much as this policy seems to absurdly defy the logic of all the rightwing politicians getting elected through their tax cuts rhetoric and austerity programs, the truth becomes apparent that the tens of thousands spent on prisoners goes to line the pockets of big developers, construction firms, and prison management companies.

The jails are clogged with people who are in jail mainly because they are poor, addicted, and/or Native. Of charges that came to court in Canada in 2008-2009 about 21% were for administrative 'crimes' such as failure to appear in court, breach of probation (missing an appointment with your probation officer), or failure to comply with an order such as a no-go in a certain area. These charges are often generated as a consequence of drug charges, especially possession charges, that are later dropped because they are unlikely to result in any serious sanction. They are crimes that someone with the resources to keep track of court appointments, get to court and have representation would never do time for. Another 7% are drug possession and trafficking charges with no suggestion of violent behaviour, basically prohibition charges. And another 23% are for crimes against property, again with no suggestion of violence. From survival shoplifting to break-and-enter to auto theft, these are mainly crimes of economic survival generated by the gross inequality and poverty of our society. Only 12% of reported crimes in Canada are considered violent. A 1988 report on young offenders in custody in Manitoba shows that 45% were incarcerated for property crimes, 7.6% for 'crimes against themselves' such as drug use, sexual immorality or public drunkenness and fully 26.5% were in jail for victimless crimes like failure to appear in court.[12]

---

[12] For a longer analysis, including mass incarceration as a successor system to residential schools, see my article *The Mass Incarceration Agenda* at http://basicsnews.ca/2011/12/the-mass-incarceration-agenda-in-canada-the-view-from-vancouver/

THE NEW REGIME OF SOCIAL CONTROL

While the institutional influence of the police and the profit takers from the Prison Industrial Complex are certainly factors in shaping the current trend toward criminalization and mass incarceration of the poor, it would be a mistake to view these as the decisive factors. This shift, like neoliberalism itself, is not a policy of any particular politician or government, but rather a set of ideologies, policies and practices linked to the political consensus within the ruling class about how to maximize the rate of exploitation and manage the smooth-running of the system.

The transition from the 'welfare state' regime of social control (through integrative, redistributive and indoctrination programs) to the neoliberal regime of social control (through criminalization, police and prisons) has been cleverly described as the capitalist state shifting from its left hand to its right. This description is apt in the sense that it insists on the continuity of the capitalist state and identifies the regime of social control as instrumental—a strategy for maintaining the dominances of the capitalist ruling class and maximizing profit within a particular context. What is important to keep in mind, and what the metaphor doesn't necessarily expose, is that the context is shaped by class struggle—and decisively by revolutionary class struggle and the threat to the capitalist system as a whole. Militant class struggles in Canada, Europe and the U.S. won important concessions from capital including the economic and political 'rights' that became the basis for the welfare state. But more importantly, it was the workers and peasants of Russia and China who, by making revolution and expropriating the capitalists in their countries, and who (given growing communist-led people's struggles across the world) created the global political context for a 'kinder, gentler' capitalism in the core capitalist countries. Absent the threat of revolution and a concrete alternative social system, and faced with its own crisis of overproduction, neoliberalism is decisively the strategy of the capitalist ruling class, and no amount of liberal hand wringing, pointing to it's irrationality or even mass reformist social movements are likely to change that.

Punishing the poor is the weapon that the ruling class uses to justify it's current policy regime, to solidify its control over the 'middle class' in a time of instability and shrinking economic prospects for the 'middle strata' (by fostering fear, creating an enemy) and to encourage a compliant working class by making the prospect of economic failure more scary and thus the desire for economic stability/security—even if wages and working conditions are worsening—all the more urgent.

Pick a bigger weapon...

The resistance that we build to police harassment and violence and to mass incarceration in our communities is important. And there is a great deal to be learned from the VANDU campaign which has been dogged in exposing and opposing the Vancouver Police Department and in fighting for reforms that redistribute both wealth and power away from the police and to our communities. But while community campaigns can make small gains and give us glimpses of an alternative to the police/mass incarceration state, they will not turn the tide in this global context of economic, environmental, and social crisis.

A cross-country campaign against criminalization and mass incarceration could be an important next step. This would give us a chance to share information about the similarities and differences of how this agenda is being implemented in poor communities across Canada and could amplify our voice in exposing and opposing these policies at the level of the federal government.

But we shouldn't harbour any illusions that this is a democratic process, or that the ruling class will (or *can*, for that matter) retreat from these policies just because we make a fuss. Ultimately we need to "pick a bigger weapon", and challenge the whole system if we are ever going to achieve respect, justice and dignity for poor people and our communities.

Tears 4 Justice and the Missing and Murdered Women and Children Across Canada: An Interview with Gladys Radek

BY VICKI CHARTRAND

We acknowledge the Traditional Custodians of this land, on this Algonquin territory and Turtle Island. We acknowledge and pay our respects to the elders both past and present.

BACKGROUND

On December 6, 2012, the National Action Day to End Violence Against Women, I interviewed Gladys Radek in Ottawa, Ontario. Gladys is from the Gitksan Wet'suwet'en territory, more commonly known as Moricetown, British Columbia. She recently moved from Vancouver to Ottawa, or to the 'belly of the beast' as Gladys suggests, to continue her work raising awareness of the missing and murdered women and children across Canada. Gladys is a human rights and grassroots activist who began organizing when her niece, Tamara Lynn Chipman, went missing on September 21, 2005 in Prince Rupert, B.C. along Highway 16—infamously known as the Highway of Tears. Tamara was 22 years old and mother to a 4-year-old boy when she disappeared—she is still missing today.

Gladys' work began with the Walk 4 Justice on June 21, 2008, walking from Vancouver to Ottawa. Since then, Gladys has co-organized 4 more walks across Canada to continue raising awareness nation wide on the far too many missing and murdered women and to support the families who have lost loved ones. Her fifth and final walk, the Tears 4 Justice walk,

113

began in Halifax on June 21, 2013 and ended in Prince Rupert on September 21, 2013—approximately 7,500 kilometers over the course of 105 days. Throughout her walks, Gladys has met many families and has collected the names of over 4,200 missing and murdered women and children across Canada, with a large majority being Aboriginal women and girls. Gladys, and other supporters, are pushing for a National Grassroots Symposium with the families of the missing and murdered women and children, a National Public Inquiry that explores the systemic gendered and racialized realities of these disappearances, and the development of a unified National Action Plan that will protect women and children in this country. The ultimate goal is to eliminate all forms of violence against women and children but, as Gladys states, "we need action today, tomorrow and forever to protect the life givers of our society."

This interview took place at the time of the Independent Commission of Inquiry into Policing in British Columbia (2012), also known as the Opal Commission—an inquiry into the missing and murdered women and the discriminatory conduct of the Vancouver police. The Commission was, however, fraught with inadequacies from the onset as outlined in Bennett, et al. (2012) *Blueprint for an Inquiry: Learning from the Failures of the Missing Women Commission of Inquiry.* Problems included the tendency to consult with professionals rather than with the women and families, a lack of legal funding and representation for the Aboriginal and anti-violence interveners and the families, a long drawn out and expensive inquiry that has left many questions unanswered, the undertaking of an individualistic inquiry rather than a substantive or systemic understanding of policing practices, sexism, racism, and poverty, and ultimately legitimating the violence as somehow inevitable, and finally significant conflicts of interest that, for example, saw the appointment of a Commissioner who, as Attorney General of BC, saw no value in a commission of inquiry.

According to the Opal Commission (2012) and other reports (e.g. Amnesty International, 2004; Standing Committee on the Status of Women, 2011), when it comes to police reporting and practices, there are many discrepancies, inconsistencies, and inadequacies in the recording, sharing of information and acting on missing persons cases and reports of violence. Despite this, the RCMP nonetheless contest the numbers of missing and murdered women. Recently, the RCMP questioned the 582 number of cases advanced by the Native Women's Association of Canada (NWAC) collected through their 'Sisters in Spirit'[1] campaign beginning in 2004 (NWAC, 2009; 2010),[2] claiming they only had 64 reports of the 118 names provided. Despite these conflicting accounts, NWAC's funding to further research missing and murdered indigenous women was cut in 2011 and was redirected to an RCMP non-distinctive database for missing persons. This approach effectively removes any gendered and racialized understanding from the analysis and offers little context and understanding to the disappearances of Aboriginal women or women in general. Thus far, Saskatchewan appears to be the only province to have carried out a systemic review of missing persons and found 60% were Aboriginal women. The most recent government work carried out with particular reference to Aboriginal women is by Statistics Canada (2011) in their report *Violent Victimization of Aboriginal Women in the Canadian Provinces, 2009*. The report reveals that close to 67,000 Aboriginal women aged 15 or older living in the Canadian provinces reported being the victim of violence in the previous 12 months. According to the *General Social Survey (GSS) on Victimization*, the overall rate of self-reported violent victimization among Aboriginal women was almost three times higher than the rate of violent victimization reported by non-Aboriginal women. These numbers are, of course, limited to their methodology such as with an inability to reach remote and transient indigenous populations, to engage indigenous participation and the extreme lack of trust between indigenous peoples

---

[1] The Sisters in Spirit campaign was later renamed Evidence to Action, as requested by the federal government to ensure continued 8 month funding of the project. Of the 582 cases from 1980 to 2010, 115 (20%) involve missing women and girls, 393 (67%) involve women or girls who died as the result of homicide or negligence, and 21 cases (4%) fall under the category of suspicious. There are 53 cases (9%) where the nature of the case remains unknown, meaning it is unclear whether the woman was murdered, is missing or died in suspicious circumstances.

[2] Ivison, John, "Conflicting numbers on missing aboriginal women another reason an inquiry is needed", *National Post*, 19, February 2013.

and a colonial government. There are countless stories and cases that remain untold.

Canada's Royal Commission Report on Aboriginal Peoples (1996) thoroughly documents how every aspect of Aboriginal peoples lives has been governed from education, status, wages, employment and so on. The *Report of the Aboriginal Justice Inquiry of Manitoba, Commission into the Death of Helen Betty Osborne* (1999) reveals, among other things, an implicit but decisive belief Aboriginal women and their bodies are accessible. Most of the public and the criminal justice system hold the view that women are responsible for their own safety and ultimately for the violence committed against them. In such a climate of impunity, women are reluctant to go to the police who often see such violence as a normal and acceptable part of the women's' lives. Few police forces in Canada have concrete guidelines to help officers evaluate the risks to missing persons and what kind of investigation is required. According to Amnesty's report *No More Stolen Sisters* (2009) women, and particularly Aboriginal women, are made vulnerable through:

> 1) the role of racism and misogyny; 2) the sharp disparities in economic, social, political and cultural rights; 3) the continued disruption of Indigenous societies caused by the historic and ongoing mass removal of children from Indigenous families and communities; 4) the disproportionately high number of Indigenous women in Canadian prisons, many of whom are themselves the victims of violence and abuse; and 5) inadequate police response to violence against Indigenous women as illustrated by the handling of missing persons cases (4).

On February 19, 2013, a Special Committee On Missing and Murdered Indigenous Women and Girls was created—a parliamentary inquiry of investigation specific to missing and murdered Aboriginal women. The decision to create the committee came a day after Human Rights Watch (2013), an international watchdog organization, launched their report, Those *Who Take Us Away: Abusive Policing and Failures in Protection of Indigenous Women and Girls in Northern British Columbia*—a scathing report citing allegations of abusive police practices, brutality, assaults and rape of indigenous and other dispossessed women by RCMP officers in Northern BC. Among many things, the report outlines the lack of trust between state officials and Aboriginal women.

Women who call the police for help may find themselves blamed for the abuse, are at times shamed for alcohol or substance use, and risk arrest for actions taken in self-defense (10).

Not only are Aboriginal women less likely to report incidents of violence, but also fear experiencing further violence at the hands of the police. According to Amnesty International Canada (2004) *Stolen Sisters: A Human Rights Response to Discrimination and Violence Against Indigenous Women in Canada*, families described how the police fail to act when sisters or daughters go missing, how families are treated with disrespect and are not informed about the investigation, if there is any investigation.

There have been grassroots initiatives in place to better support families and track the occurrences of missing and murdered women. Operation Thunderbird[3] uses crowd mapping to document the murders, assaults and disappearances of women in Canada and the United States. Ka Ni Kanichihk, a non-profit organization, has provided an online toolkit for Missing Persons.[4] Missing Manitoba Women[5] carry out searches and support families in finding loved ones. Ending the Violence Against Women, BC (2011) also released a report and toolkit entitled *Increasing Safety for Aboriginal Women*.

Over the years, other reports, research, symposiums, recommendations for women and Aboriginal women in particular include the Highway of Tears Symposium (2006) *A Collective Voice for the Victims Who Have Been Silenced*; Status of Women Canada's (2006) *Summary of the Policy Forum on Aboriginal Women and Violence*; Coordinating Committee of Senior Officials, (Criminal) Missing Women Working Group (2010; 2012) *Report and Recommendations in Issues Related to the High Number of Murdered and Missing Women in Canada*; Status of Women Canada's (2011) *Ending Violence Against Aboriginal Women and Girls*; and the Canadian Feminist Alliance for International Action's (2012) *Disappearances and Murders of Aboriginal Women and Girls in Canada*. What

[3] https://missingsisters.crowdmap.com/main

[4] http://www.kanikanichihk.ca/?page_id=761

[5] https://www.facebook.com/MissingManitobaWomen

these reports reveal, among many things, is the need for a nationally coordinated and organized action plan that addresses the endemic issues of poverty, sexism and racism that heighten the conditions for violence to occur, address current colonial practices of segregation like child welfare and imprisonment, and to implement practical programs and supports, such as shelters and transportation, that will alleviate those conditions that force individuals into dangerous situations.

Despite longstanding recommendations, documentation, reporting, and research that has been undertaken, there is still little specifically done to address the gendered and racialized reality of the disappearances and murders of women and children. To date the government has not launched a national investigation and has refused to develop a National Action plan,[6] despite such plans existing elsewhere such as in Australia (see Council of Australian Government, 2010). The Special Committee On Missing and Murdered Indigenous Women and Girls (2012) stated that what is required is a co-ordinated, holistic approach to violence. The vulnerability of women and Aboriginal women is not new; it is chronic.

INTERVIEW

Vicki: What made you decide to walk across Canada to raise awareness of the missing and murdered women and children?

Gladys: I started the Walk 4 Justice back in 2008. Growing up in Northern BC, I often knew about women going missing or being murdered, especially in the Aboriginal communities. I was tired that nothing was actually being done. It also really resonated for me when my niece, Tamara Chipman, went missing in 2005 and how little support the family received from the police from the onset.

Walking from community to community seemed like a good way to unite families and supporters and raise awareness to the ongoing violence against women nation wide. Walking the highways across Canada is also significant given that it is the

---

[6]Kilpatrick, Sean, "No action plan on missing aboriginal women: Protesters rally for missing, abused aboriginal women", Canadian Press, 5 July 2011.

highways where many of the women's bodies are being 'dumped'. As we walked across Canada, we met many other family members who were experiencing grave injustices for many years at the hands of the police who were not investigating the reports of disappearances, who were not helping families in their search for their missing loved ones, and who were not offering much support or information to the families.

Unfortunately, as Aboriginal women, this is also something longstanding in our history; something we are very familiar with. I was raised in several communities along the Highway of Tears (Highway 16), so it has been a part of my whole life. Walking the highways lets us connect with the families, hear their stories and support them—that's grassroots. It is difficult to appreciate how this impacts families and communities unless it is happening to you or you are in it. Many of my relatives have gone missing or have been murdered, whether it is from my foster family or biological family. This really is something many of us are familiar with. So I walk.

Vicki: Explain to us why it is so important to work from a grassroots level. What advantages does a grassroots approach have in addressing this issue?

Gladys: Grassroots lets you connect with those who are either directly or immediately impacted. When I advertised the walk, I had an immediate response from the families. Despite what the police say, we hear firsthand from the families that whenever they report a loved one missing, they are often told by the police that she 'might be out partying' or she may have 'run away'. The families are more often than not told they will have to wait 24, 48, 72 hours, or sometimes longer before the police will act. Sometimes the police insinuate it is the fault of the families because maybe 'they had a fight with their daughter'. Some of the families won't even report because there may be charges pending, or the police suggest that the women are trying to evade their charges by running away. That is what happened in this situation of my niece Tamara who has been missing. The police have a 'blame the victim' attitude. The problem is sexism and racism and the racist relations with the police and government.

Vicki: In recent news reports, the police have been contesting that the number of Aboriginal women who are missing or murdered is as high as 582, as advanced by the Native Women's Association of Canada.

Gladys: How could they? I do not know how they can. We have the names of over 4200 women who are missing and murdered, with the majority being Aboriginal women. The police are not doing what is needed. In many ways they promote the violence and racism by picking and choosing who gets to be considered as 'deserving' victims. Statistics can also be a problem. Statistics are used to confuse or dally around the problem. There are women going missing and murdered. It is tiring how we are simply arguing over numbers. The police are just not responding. Publicly they will tell you that they are immediately responding and that the 24 hour wait period is a myth, but many communities are having to put together their own search parties. The reality is that it is a network of community and people that respond to the disappearances of women that is more helpful and effective. Despite their efforts, the communities lack the resources and funds to keep on the searches, while the police have all the resources.

Vicki: In my experiences, the justice system tends to minimize the extent of the problem by making violence an individual problem when it is clearly endemic to Canada. It fails to break down attitudes of violence while criminalizing those who are most vulnerable and coming from poverty. Do you have a sense that the police are trying to minimize the problem?

Gladys: Absolutely. There is no accountability. When you don't have accountability, you don't have justice, you don't have closure, and you don't have equality. The problem only gets bigger. Until we have accountability from the police, they should not be a part of the solution. The police first need to admit that they are a big part of the problem.

Vicki: What concerns do you have with the Opal Commission that is currently investigating the police conduct around reports and their investigation into the missing and murdered women in Vancouver?[7]

Gladys: They are not consulting with the families, especially with first nations women. They only invited some families to the commission, but not all the families. For example, only the families of the six victims that Robert Pickton was convicted of murdering were invited. There are many more, and although it may be hard, you need to give time to all the families. All this is going to lead to just another report. Like with so many of the existing reports, it's people asking the same questions to the same people. For example, the RCMP are reporting that they have many programs to address this issue, but if these programs were working, then why are we still having so many women going missing? We do not need any more reports. We have the recommendations from the Highway of Tears Symposium, the Native Women's Association of Canada and Amnesty International. We have the recommendations. We need a national action plan. We need to implement programs that are holistic and culturally sensitive and that have eliminating violence as the basis of its framework. We need community, healing and native friendship centres. We need places that teach about violence, culture, and tradition. We need safe places and safe travel. We need places that can remove people away form violence and problems. We need shelter, safety, support and healing.

Vicki: In my work in the anti-violence field, governments are more and more trying to make violence against women a housing issue. Although housing is important, the tendency is to undermine the systemic and endemic violence occurring against women and children nationally and worldwide. This only heightens the potential for more violence to occur.

Gladys: There is no doubt it is a violence issue. We are holding the government, police and justice system to account for this vi-

---

[7] Editor's note: The Commission concluded in 2012.

olence. We want for everyone to have a roof over their heads, food in their bellies and safe place to stay. Right now there is a lot of pain in our societies. It does not matter what society you come from. We need to heal. We need to overcome the pain and developing on a violence-free future. I feel like I have been in mourning since I began this journey, but I am proud of all the walkers who keep raising awareness in their own communities.

Vicki: Can you give us a day in the life of a walker?

Gladys: One day we were walking just outside Portage la Prairie. There was a young woman who had just been reported missing as we were walking through the territory and we offered to help search for her. The mother was very thankful for our offer, but she wanted us to keep on our walk and continue raising awareness for the women. But she asked us as we continued our walk to "keep your noses in the air". That statement didn't press upon me until later. As we continued on our walk, we got a smell of death in the air. The smell of death is something you will never forget. It was our worst fear. We were afraid that we were going to find the young women's body. Unlike when you are driving, when you are walking on the side of the road, you see things and as we walked along, we saw a black hoodie. This young woman had been reported to be wearing a black hoodie when she was last seen. That scared the hell out of me; it scared the hell out of all of us. My granddaughter, three other walkers, and I started combing through the grass around the area. After about a half hour of smelling death and this young woman on our minds, we were relieved to have eventually found the carcass of a deer. But there are no words that can express how sickening the feeling was for that half-hour of searching for her with the smell of death in our nostrils. It touched on all of us. We are the ones who have lost. We are the one's who feel the pain. We know what we have lost. We know the pain. We also know the resources we need. We know.

Vicki: What does colonialism look like to you today?

Gladys: They haven't won yet. We're still here. We're still here and were still strong as ever. We are fewer in numbers and unless we bring things back into the grassroots heritage and our knowledge of ancestry, we will lose that. It is still genocide. I do not feel bad about using that word. When you take away our women and children that is genocide. If you think about how the average Aboriginal women has 5 children, and how we have collected at least 3000 names of Aboriginal women who have gone missing or who have been murdered, that's 15,0000 first generation children we've lost. It is a silent genocide.

Many people don't understand either their culture or colonialism and we are also receiving mixed messages. Like receiving cultural training, in a prison environment. It is a contradiction in terms. Aboriginal people have been devalued. We are also trained as sex toys as a result of colonialism. This is why I see the legalizing of prostitution as problematic. We are building laws that implicitly lead us to believe that we are responsible for serving the wants of men, or what are often considered 'needs'. It confuses people. It not only leads us to believe that we somehow have this obligation, but it also more and more becomes the only means by which women, and especially Aboriginal women, can make money, live or survive. This does not protect women—it only further entrenches women in an industry that has always been and is still obviously inherently violent, again particularly for the majority of Aboriginal women who are poor. Many of the women that are picked up on the highway of tears and killed, are seen as accessible or available for sex. The men believe they have a right to own and do as they will with women to satisfy their 'needs'. That is why the legalizing of prostitution is dangerous.[8] It leads men to believe that they have even more entitlement and access to women's bodies. Many of these so-called 'managers' of women prey on vulnerable women and entice them into prostitution either forcibly, or preying on their wants, needs, fears and desires. Legalizing prostitution will make it easier to bring more vulnerable women into this industry and there will be even fewer choices available for women to make a viable living otherwise. It is possible that decriminalizing prostitution will serve specif-

---

[8] Editor's note: This does not reflect the views of the Radical Criminology editors.

ic type of women, and more often women who are privileged. It will also drive the prices down for those women who are trying to survive with more women 'freely' entering the trade. I don't think this is a simple black and white debate. We need to acknowledge the vulnerabilities inherent in our system and that the 'law' will not simply shift that—when in fact the law has always been implicit in perpetuating vulnerabilities. We cannot ignore that.

Vicki: What do you want people to know?

Gladys: We want people to know that Canada is guilty of crimes against humanity. It is a safe haven for violence against women.

Vicki: From the people to the people.

Gladys: Right. What do we want? Justice! When do we want it? Now!

REFERENCES

Aboriginal Justice Inquiry of Manitoba. (1991). *Report of the Aboriginal Justice Inquiry of Manitoba: The Deaths of Helen Betty Osborne and John Joseph Harper*. Winnipeg: The Aboriginal Justice Implementation Commission. http://www.ajic.mb.ca/volume.html (August 6, 2013).

Amnesty International Canada. 2004. *Stolen Sisters: A Human Rights Response to Discrimination and Violence Against Indigenous Women in Canada*. Ottawa. http://www.amnesty.ca/sites/default/files/amr20003 2004enstolensisters.pdf (August 2, 2013).

Amnesty International Canada. 2009. *No More Stolen Sisters: The Need for a Comprehensive Response to Discrimination and Violence Against Indigenous Women in Canada*. Ottawa. http://ywcacanada.ca/data/research_docs/00000021.pdf (August 2, 2013).

Bennett, Darcie, David Eby, Kasari Govender, and Katrina Pacey. 2012. *Blueprint for an Inquiry: Learning from the Failures of the Missing Women Commission of Inquiry*. Vancouver: B.C. Civil Liberties Association, West Coast Women's Legal Education and Action Fund,

Pivot Legal Society. http://www.westcoastleaf.org/userfiles/file/Missing%20Women%20Commission%20of%20Inquiry%20joint%20report%202012.pdf (August 2, 2013).

Canada, Report of the Royal Commission on Aboriginal Peoples. 1996. Five Volumes.

Ottawa: Minister of Supply and Services. http://www.collectionscanada.gc.ca/webarchives/20071115053257/ http://www.ainc-inac.gc.ca/ch/rcap/sg/sgmm_e.html (August 6, 2013).

Canadian Feminist Alliance for International Action. 2012. *Disappearances and Murders of Aboriginal Women and Girls in Canada: Submission to the United Nations on the Elimination of Racial Discrimination*. Ottawa. http://fafia-afai.org/wp-content/uploads/2011/06/FAFIACERD submissionfinalJan252012.pdf (August 2, 2013).

Coordinating Committee of Senior Officials, (Criminal) Missing Women Working Group. 2010. *Report and Recommendations in Issues Related to the High Number of Murdered and Missing Women in Canada, September 2010.* FPT Deputy Ministers Responsible for Justice. http://www.scics.gc.ca/CMFiles/830992005_e1MAJ-2112011-6827.pdf (August 2, 2013).

Coordinating Committee of Senior Officials, (Criminal) Missing Women Working Group. 2012. *Report and Recommendations in Issues Related to the High Number of Murdered and Missing Women in Canada, January 2012.* FPT Deputy Ministers Responsible for Justice. http://www.justice.gov.sk.ca/adx/aspx/adxGetMedia.aspx?DocID=3025,104,81,1,Documents&MediaID=45139809-994e-4788-99f4-f5e24b3af11b&Filename=FPT-missing-women-report-2012.pdf (August 6, 2013).

Council of Australian Government. 2010. *The National Plan to Reduce Violence against Women and their Children 2010 – 2022* http://www.fahcsia.gov.au/sites/default/files/documents/05_2012/national_plan.pdf (August 6, 2013).

Ending the Violence Against Women, BC. 2011. Increasing Safety for Aboriginal Women: Key Themes and Resources. Vancouver. http://www.endingviolence.org/files/uploads/boriginal_Women_-_themes_and_resource_May_12.pdf (August 2, 2013).

Highway of Tears Symposium. 2006. *A Collective Voice for the Victims Who Have Been Silenced: Highway of Tears Symposium Recommendation Report*. Prince George. http://www.ubcic.bc.ca/files/PDF/highwayoftearsfinal.pdf (August 2, 2013).

Human Rights Watch. 2013. *Those Who Take Us Away: Abusive Policing and Failures in Protection of Indigenous Women and Girls in Northern British Columbia, Canada & USA*. http://www.hrw.org/sites/default/files/reports/canada0213webwcover.pdf (August 2, 2013).

Justice for Girls. 2005. *Justice System's Response: Violence against Aboriginal Girls.* Vancouver. http://www.justiceforgirls.org/publications/pdfs/Violence%20against%20Aboriginal%20Girls%20-%20Final%20Brief%20-%20Sept%202005.pdf (August 2, 2013).

Native Women's Association of Canada. 2009. *Voices of Our Sisters In Spirit: A Report to Families and Communities, 2nd Edition.* Ottawa. (August 2, 2013). http://www.nwac.ca/sites/default/files/download/admin/NWAC_Voicesof OurSistersInSpiritII_March2009FINAL.pdf (August 2, 2013).

Native Women's Association of Canada. 2010. *What Their Stories Tell Us: Research Findings from the Sisters In Spirit Initiative.* Ottawa. http://ywcacanada.ca/data/research_docs/00000136.pdf (August 2, 2013).

Oppal, Honourable Wally T., QC Commissioner. 2012. *Forsaken: The Report of the Missing Women Commission of Inquiry.* Vancouver. http://www.missingwomeninquiry.ca (August 6, 2013).

Pacific Association of First Nations Women, Ending Violence Association of BC and BC Women's Hospital & Health. 2005. *Researched to Death: B.C. Aboriginal Women and Violence.* Vancouver. http://www.endingviolence.org/files/uploads/Researched_To_Death_Final _2005.pdf (August 6, 2013).

Statistics Canada. 2011. *Violent Victimization of Aboriginal Women in the Canadian Provinces, 2009.* Ottawa. http://www.statcan.gc.ca/pub/85-002-x/2011001/article/11439-eng.pdf (August 6, 2013).

Status of Women Canada. 2006. *Summary of the Policy Forum on Aboriginal Women and Violence: Building Safe and Healthy Families and Communities, March 27-28, 2006, at Ottawa.* http://humanservices.alberta.ca/documents/aboriginal-women-forum-english.pdf (August 2, 2013).

Status of Women Canada. 2011. Ending Violence Against Aboriginal Women and Girls: Report of the Standing Committee on the Status of Women. Ottawa. http://www.parl.gc.ca/content/hoc/Committee/411 /FEWO/Reports/RP5322860/feworp01/feworp01-e.pdf (August 2, 2013).

[book reviews]

Drawing the Line Once Again: Paul Goodman's Anarchist Writings
Paul Goodman
(San Francisco: PM Press, 2010. 128 pages.)

Reviewed by—Jeff Shantz,
Kwantlen Polytechnic University, Dec 2013

Despite the fact that anarchist theorists (from major figures like Peter Kropotkin and Emma Goldman to other lesser known writers and activists) have been actively involved in developing criminological perspectives and practices from the inception of the discipline, much of anarchism has been written out of the histories of criminology. Thus, the significant contributions of anarchism to criminology have been overlooked or forgotten. More recently the important undertakings of newer scholars such as Christopher Howell have contributed to the archeology of criminological knowledge and uncovered crucial contributions of anarchism.

The overlooking of anarchism has meant that important voices have been silenced or remain unheard. Among the more interesting recent commentators has been Paul Goodman. While Goodman is generally recognized as one of the most important and influential inspirations of the New Left during the 1960s and 1970s, it is probably true that very few people associate his ideas with criminology.

Goodman's work addresses a range of issues of criminological concern, from causes of social harms through critical analysis of responses to crime. His work prefigures recent developments in peacemaking criminology and restorative justice. The recent collection *Drawing the Line Once Again* offers a fine introduction the Goodman's criminological analysis, offering an outline of his communal anarchist criminology.

Goodman speaks against the proliferation of laws and penalties, covering issues that are neither crimes nor socially harmful, and such encroachments on judiciary autonomy as mandatory sentencing and differential punishments—largely linked to race in the US. In his criticism of moral regulation, he notes that most (ever-expanding) laws of managed societies are addressed toward the concerns of power rather real threats. In his view: "Many (I believe most) of the so-called crimes are really free acts whose repression causes our timidity; natural society has a far shorter list of crimes" (Goodman 2009, 47).

Goodman argues that the distinction between "political prisoners" and "common criminals" is false. The common criminal has likely committed a political crime. Moral and property relations under capitalism are, as Goodman suggests, "unthinkable without the prison system" (cited in Stoehr 2010, 11). As Goodman editor, and longtime colleague, Taylor Stoehr suggests, the prisons are largely reserved for those who do not conform to the coercive social order, usually determined by poverty, class, racialism (2010, 14).

Goodman notes that the state permits "moral vices that fit well into the commodity system" while jailing people for expressing pleasures outside the system of exchange or that undermine the social discipline...thus, one may not steal, copulate in the park, or encourage the sexuality of children" (2009, 51). He concludes: "We must proceed on the assumption that the coercive society knows well which acts are a threat to it and which are not" (2009, 51).

Notably, Goodman does not speak of penal reform. He, more fundamentally, questions why prisons are allowed to exist period. Indeed, he includes the penal system along with the military industries as the areas most urgently requiring cuts in public spending.

Goodman suggests that in asylums, around ninety percent are harmless and there is no need to confine them at all. In prisons, there is no point in confining the large percent who have committed one time crimes. These include crimes of passion, familial crimes. In his view, people should atone for the harm they have caused and get through their guilt, but this can be done and is more likely to be successful if they are accepted back into the community rather than if they are isolated and made desperate (Goodman 2011, 91).

There is little evidence that punishing some deters others. Most who do not engage in crimes such as theft or shoplifting, forgery, and so on do not do so because of their lifestyle and informal influences rather than formal legal risks or threatened punishments (Goodman 2011, 91). In this, Goodman's insights resonate with well developed theories in criminology such as the differential association theory of Edwin Sutherland and the social control theory of Travis Hirschi which provide similar explanations.

For Goodman, there is little evidence that we know how to rehabilitate or correct deviants within current dominant institutions of criminal justice. In the end prisons and asylums are "enclaves of the indigestible" and managed society simply seeks to keep "the whole mess out of sight" (2011, 91).

Goodman opposes views, such as those in classical criminology or more recently rational choice theories, which view crime as the outcome of rational calculation, or assessment of costs and benefits. For Goodman:

> The chief reason that so-called "moral legislation" has no influence in deterring vices is that temptation to the vices does not occur in the same psychological context as rational calculation of legal risks —unlike business fraud or risking a parking ticket. And it is likely that much authentic criminal behavior is compulsive in the same way. (2011, 91)

According to Goodman, the notion of exacting revenge for crime is an irrational and superstitious fantasy (2010, 117). Those who transgress the law have a share of the social world as their birthright (Goodman 2011, 92). His is an approach that speaks to, and in some ways prefigures, contemporary versions of restorative justice. The restorative justice approaches, even if not directly influenced by anarchism, reflect a "recurrent human impulse" (Goodman 2011, 92).

For Stoehr, alternatives, despite recent developments, have proved difficult for people, from criminologists, to legislative representatives, to regular citizens, to entertain largely "because the entire realm of crime and punishment has so long been accepted as the sole prerogative of the State and its apparatus (2010, 18). It is the state that establishes, sets, and carries out the functions of law, procedure, and punishment. Indeed, crime is viewed and treated not as a transgression against a person or community but as a transgression against the state.

For an anarchist approach, the administering of true justice requires that all parties have a voice that is heard and assessed in face to face contact. Human expression and feeling must be respected (in a way the courts will not allow). For Stoehr:

> In today's hectic criminal courts the victim has almost as little say as the offender, often not even testifying in court, while the community is "represented" by an array of state officials. The central roles are played by hired experts, the prosecuting attorney and the defendant's often state-appointed counsel, who also has an official role to play. Judge and jury listen to a drama in which the real character and history of all the important actors is almost totally unknown, and regarded as irrelevant. No one speaks for humanity. (2010, 18)

The criminal justice system is a prime example of the managed society and the state power which treats people as objects and things rather than human beings. In this, Goodman echoes C. Wright Mills' concerns about the "thingification" of humans and human social relations within liberal democratic capitalism.

"War is the health of the state," as Randolph Bourne has suggested. For Goodman, modern history in fact teaches no other lesson, from the personalistic wars of the sixteenth and seventeenth centuries to recent economic and geopolitical wars (2010, 114). In the ultramodern period, this lesson has been extended in the various social wars (against poverty, drugs, terror). His work provides keen insights into the character and content of these developing battles.

□ ◊ □□ ◊ □□ ◊ □

SUPPORT POLITICAL PRISONERS

**Check the web for local groups
doing prisoner support in your area...**

prisonjustice.ca
abcf.net &
    BristolABC.wordpress.com
    DenverABC.wordpress.com
    GuelphABC.noblogs.org
    TorontoABC.wordpress.com
4strugglemag.org
supportmariemason.org
supporteric.org

FELLOW WORKERS:

Remember!

WE ARE IN HERE FOR YOU; YOU ARE OUT THERE FOR US

GDC

www.supporteric.org

Books 2 PRISONERS

PRISONJUSTICE.CA

Radical Criminology, a new journal of theory and practice for struggle

Considering contributing to an upcoming issue?

Authors are encouraged to submit articles for publication, directly to our website: **http://journal.radicalcriminology.org**

We are actively seeking marginalized voices, not only in the field of critical criminological scholarship, but also artists, activists, and reviewers. Or, send us a letter!

All academic articles are subject to a blind peer review process. (This does not include "insurgencies," artwork, poetry and book reviews, which will be assessed by our editorial committee.)

Please visit our website for more detailed submission guidelines. (There are no submission nor publication fees.) Create a reader and author account there now...

We use the Public Knowledge Project's 'open journal' online submission system (http://pkp.sfu.ca/ojs), which allows authors to submit papers via the Web. This system speeds up the submission and review process, and allows you to view the status of your paper online.

Artwork, poetic submissions, and notes on insurgencies can also be posted to our website, e-mailed to <editors@radicalcriminology.org> or send us mail at:
Radical Criminology,
ATTN: Jeff Shantz, Dept. of Criminology,
Kwantlen Polytechnic University
12666 72nd Ave,
Surrey, B.C. V3W 2M8

(and on twitter...find us @critcrim)

www.ingramcontent.com/pod-product-compliance
Lightning Source LLC
Chambersburg PA
CBHW050655270326
41927CB00012B/3034